The Fujita Plan

The Fujita Plan

Mark Felton

Pen & Sword
MILITARY

First published in Great Britain in 2006 by
Pen & Sword Military
an imprint of
Pen & Sword Books Ltd
47 Church Street
Barnsley
South Yorkshire
S70 2AS

ISBN 1 844 154 807

A CIP catalogue record for this book is available from the British Library

Typeset in 11/13 Sabon by
Lamorna Publishing Services

Printed and bound in England by
Biddles Ltd.

For a complete list of Pen & Sword titles please contact
PEN & SWORD BOOKS LIMITED
47 Church Street, Barnsley, South Yorkshire, S70 2AS, England
E-mail: enquiries@pen-and-sword.co.uk
Website: www.pen-and-sword.co.uk

Dedicated with love to Fang Fang

Contents

Introduction

The 'Fujita Plan' is named for a fairly minor member of Japan's wartime armed services, a man who was not even an officer. Chief Warrant Officer (Flying) Nobuo Fujita, a former test pilot in the Imperial Japanese Navy conceived a plan of such daring and such possible rewards for Japan's arms that its worth was immediately seized upon by far more senior officers who perhaps enjoyed Fujita's boldness that was in the finest traditions of the *samurai*. The plan was Fujita's, but the eventual missions that the pilot undertook were the product of careful planning involving even a member of the Japanese royal family, and the mission was simple: to bomb the mainland of the United States. The 'Fujita Plan' is the title of this book, but it is more than just an examination a single navy pilot's unique missions over the United States, the book examines the often bungled efforts of the Japanese to extend the Pacific War to the very shores of the United States and Australia. Fujita provides a link between the two operations, as he was the only Japanese pilot to fly over both Australia and America during the Second World War, and his amazing idea forms the core of the story of Japan's war on the American and Australian home fronts. Many of the submarines detailed throughout the pages of this book were active at various times during 1941–43 off the coasts of the United States and Australia, often alternating patrols between the two far-flung localities. This book has drawn together the strands of these two separate but intertwined operations into a single narrative. The Japanese made half-hearted efforts to isolate both the continent of Australia and the United States west coast from external trade, they made a series of largely uncoordinated attacks on both nations, and they employed the full gamut of specialist equipment on these 'missions impossible', from two-man midget submarines to tiny submarine-launched floatplanes, balloons loaded with bombs to huge submarines surfacing offshore and unleashing shells from their deck-guns. Merchant ships were sunk or damaged as the Japanese tried to employ their submarines as commerce raiders along the coasts of Oregon and California, and all around Australia. They behaved like the world's most successful merchant ship hunters, Germany's U-boats, but failed to emulate the high kill ratios recorded by their erstwhile allies. In these operations the Japanese Navy off the coasts of the United States and Australia attempted and committed war crimes, as submarine skippers grew increasingly frustrated by their lack of success. One submarine skipper appeared to sail to California's coast thirsting for revenge against a place where he had suffered a grave loss of face before the war. While some Japanese were a disgrace to their uniform and their country, others displayed courage beyond what was expected of them at the time by their superiors, as the young men determined to infiltrate Pearl Harbor and Sydney Harbour in tiny submarines demonstrated, or to take to the skies in little floatplanes and go gallivanting over protected enemy airspace searching out secrets and targets, and nearly every man involved in these operations perished for almost no overall result for the Japanese war effort. In the case of the midget submarine raiders they had already accepted the likelihood of a one-way mission even before they boarded their tiny craft. For Fujita, long after the war was over he was to rediscover the places in Oregon he had tried so hard to destroy, and in an extraordinary act of reconciliation and friendship between himself and local Oregonians, eventually become an honoured citizen and bridge of understanding between the two cultures.

Only a few books have been written in the recent past about the Japanese submarine attacks on the United States and Australia, and they have tended to concentrate on one particular nation or the other. Australian writers have taken a particular interest in the Japanese midget submarine attacks on Sydney and the operations of submarines around the coasts of the great continent, and of particular note are the excellent *Australia Under Siege: Japanese Submarine Raiders 1942* by Steven L. Carruthers and David

Jenkins's *Battle Surface!* Focusing on the immense bravery and daring of the midget submarine crews who conducted the Pearl Harbor and Sydney attacks any student of this period of history should read Peggy Warner and Sadao Seno's emotive and well-named book *The Coffin Boats: Japanese Midget Submarine Operations in the Second World War*. For American historians Fujita's attacks and the activities of Japanese submarines along the west coast have been largely ignored in print. I have been fortunate to receive the assistance of local history groups along the west coast in attempting to reconstruct the events of 1942, notably the Port Orford Historical Society and the James Scott's excellent website *Harbor Defenses of the Columbia River During the Second World War* (www.csus.edu). For unpublished sources concerning the midget attacks on Sydney Harbour the Australian War Memorial at Canberra contains an extensive collection of reports and photographs, and I have also utilized local newspaper coverage extending to the shelling of Sydney and Newcastle by Japanese I-class submarines following the events in Sydney Harbour. For any author attempting to write about Japanese submarines and their operations during the Second World War one source above all others has consistently and reliably assisted this writer, making sure my dates, specifications, movements and skippers are all recorded correctly within the overall story. This is Bob Hackett and Sander Kingsepp's www.combinedfleet.com, a labour of love for the subject that is an invaluable reference source for researchers, filling in many of the gaps caused by the paucity of written material on Japanese submarines. Great books do exist, and no author on this subject can have failed to consult Carl Boyd and Akira Yoshida's *The Japanese Submarine Force in World War II* or Paul Dull's *A Battle History of the Imperial Japanese Navy*. For more technical information the encyclopaedic volumes *Warships of the Imperial Japanese Navy* by Jentschura, Jung and Michel, and Polmar and Carpenter's *Warships of the Imperial Japanese Navy 1904–1945* provide a mass of data invaluable to researchers.

The war on America's and Australia's doorstep has been largely forgotten over the past six decades, and even at the time it was an occasional story of local interest, but rarely a real source for concern at the highest levels of government. The fears generated by these hit-and-run tactics against inshore merchant shipping and military targets on land were unjustified with hindsight, but rumours continue to abound even to this day of dark Japanese wartime designs concerned with invading Australia or unleashing biological warfare upon the western United States. If the intention of the Japanese Navy was to unsettle the American and Australian populations who perhaps felt relatively secure far from the sounds of gunfire and bombs it succeeded. It bought for the Japanese a few alarming newspaper headlines, and the attacks by submarines and aircraft made both America and Australia strengthen their inshore defences, but the attacks did very little to assist the overall Japanese war effort.

The attacks, especially those of such daring and dash, such as the midget submarine attacks on Pearl Harbor and Sydney, Fujita's lone bombing missions over the forests of Oregon, and the five occasions when Japanese naval shells exploded on the shores of America and in the streets of Australian cities, are interesting for the simple fact of their incongruousness. That Japan should reach out so far came as a surprise to the United States and Australia at the time. To us, they are anomalies in the history of the Second World War, examples of forgotten corners of the history of that conflict, but corners still worth shining a little light into in attempts to complete the story of the war in the Pacific.

This book could not have been written without the kind assistance of the following individuals and institutions, and I would like to extend my deep thanks to you all: Brigadier Henry Wilson and the staff at Pen & Sword Books for their continued support; I would also like to thank my editor, Susan Econicoff, for her hard work. Many thanks to Bob Hackett and Sander Kingsepp for permitting me to reproduce data from their excellent website on Japanese submarines to be found at http://www.combinedfleet.com/sensuikan.htm. A great many thanks to the forum at www.uboat.net for enabling contact between myself and many submarine researchers, and for the continued excellent feedback from many contributors concerning all matters submarine. A great debt of thanks also to Rick Francona and the Port Orford Lifeboat Station, Oregon, for allowing me to reproduce details of the Fujita missions over Oregon and for their assistance in answering my questions and providing me with contacts. Many thanks to Don Kehn, Jr. for providing me with the declassified action reports of the USS *Edsall* from the National Archives (NARA) in Washington D.C. The following institutions are owed many thanks for their assistance; The Australian War Memorial; National Archives of Australia; The British Library; The National Archives (Public Record Office), Kew; The Albert Sloman Library, University of Essex; Colchester Central Library. Finally, a great many thanks to my wife Fang Fang for her undiminished support and encouragement throughout the gestation of this book, and I remain always indebted for her love and steady advice.

Shanghai

February 2006

Chapter 1

The Best Laid Plans

How courteous is the Japanese;
He always says, 'Excuse it, please.'
He climbs into his neighbor's garden,
And smiles, and says, 'I beg your pardon';
He bows and grins a friendly grin,
And calls his hungry family in;
He grins and bows a friendly bow;
'So sorry, this is my garden now.'

Ogden Nash

Thirty-one year old naval aviator Nobuo Fujita arrived at Imperial Japanese Navy Headquarters in Tokyo on 27 July 1942, fresh from flying duties aboard the submarine *I-25*. A small, compact man with cropped black hair and a determined expression set permanently upon his face as befitted his rank of chief warrant officer, the senior non-commissioned grade available to an enlisted man, he was directed immediately by an aide into a room inside the Japanese Admiralty's First Bureau (Operations) department. There he discovered several staff officers standing stiffly around a table on which was spread a large map of the Pacific Northwest region of the United States. All acknowledged the arrival of the only non-com to be invited to the meeting with curt nods of their heads and returned Fujita's formal salute before returning to their discussion over the map table. The most important officer present was of a relatively junior rank, but his position was of the highest standing and everyone naturally and obsequiously deferred to him. Commander Prince Takamatsu was the younger brother of the 'Sacred Crane', Emperor Hirohito, and although he was a senior member of the Imperial family he was also a serving naval officer. The young prince had taken a strong interest in an ingenious plan Fujita had dreamed up when whiling away the long periods of inactivity on active duty at sea; a plan that would come to be named the 'Fujita Plan' after its designer. The officers gathered in the room represented all the sections of the Imperial Navy who were interested in making Fujita's idea a reality.

Present at the table was a staff officer from the submarine service, and another who had once been a Japanese vice-consul in the American city of Seattle. Following formal introductions, the staff officer from submarines announced in a matter of fact tone, 'Fujita, we are going to have you bomb the American mainland.' As a stunned Fujita began to take on board the realization that his dream had finally become a reality, the staff officer who had lived and worked in the American northwest, the former vice-consul, fleshed out the headquarters staff's amendments to Fujita's original plan. 'You will bomb forests for us, right about here,' he said, stabbing his index finger at a position which Fujita could see lay approximately seventy-five miles north of the California state line. At this point Fujita began to realize that the high command had a different plan in mind entirely from his own brilliant idea. Fujita had carefully outlined a scheme in writing to headquarters for using the small reconnaissance floatplanes carried aboard submarines such as his own *I-25* to bomb important military targets and cities along the United States west coast, and to attack the Panama Canal, the vital artery that linked American naval forces in the Atlantic and Pacific Oceans and an important international trade route. He could see that the area indicated on the map that lay before him was devoid of any large towns or cities harbouring industrial or military targets. Perhaps noting the look of disappointment and confusion that crossed the young Fujita's face, the staff officer explained further: 'The north-western United States is full of forests. Once a blaze gets started in the deep woods, it is difficult to stop. Sometimes whole towns are destroyed.' The delivery of a small amount of incendiary bombs, it was explained, and the floatplane type fitted to many Japanese submarines, the Yokosuka E14Y1, was only capable of lifting a tiny munitions load, could potentially cause a huge conflagration.

The staff officer went further, detailing the important point of such a mission to Fujita: 'If we were to bomb these forests, it would put the enemy to much trouble. It might even cause large-scale panic, once residents knew Japan could reach out and bomb their families and homes from 5,000 miles away.' Fujita was also informed that a further outcome of such an attack could be the US Navy redeploying their Pacific Fleet to defend the American mainland, taking pressure off the Japanese elsewhere in the Pacific theatre.

Such was the final 'Fujita Plan'; a plan originally conceived to be a series of nuisance and morale-busting air raids conducted against the United States Pacific coast. Its evolution as a result of the 27 July meeting in Tokyo made the plan a far more dangerous proposition, a series of attacks, which, if successful, had the potential to devastate large swathes of the Pacific Northwest, causing immense physical and economic damage and the deployment of considerable civil defence and military forces into the area to both defend from further attacks and clear up the damage caused. The Japanese Navy proposed a firestorm campaign in which Imperial forces reached out across the wide Pacific and brought the war directly to America's doorstep. The United States had not been attacked on its home turf since a final entanglement with the British during the Napoleonic conflict termed the War of 1812.[1] So marked the most ambitious plan yet devised by the Japanese Empire to sow death and destruction upon the American public, safe in the knowledge that no country had managed to strike at their doorstep since the Republic's infancy.

The 'Fujita Plan' marks a strange and largely forgotten episode in the Pacific War, and was accompanied by much Japanese activity along the United States west coast, led by the Imperial Navy. Japanese submarines launched a campaign of attacks on coastal merchant shipping within sight of shore, submarines bombarded coastal installations with their deck-guns, and Japanese aircraft dropped bombs over American forests. At the same time, Australia was also targeted, and a further innovation, the midget submarine, was employed to penetrate Sydney Harbour and wreak havoc. But, as we shall see, the attention of the Japanese was always on the battles raging across the Pacific island chains and in south-east Asia, and the 'Fujita Plan' and its ilk amounted to nothing more than flea bites on an elephant as Japan's resources were thrown into defending their massive Empire. What is certain, however, is that although the submarine attacks on the United States and Australia did cause panic and confusion throughout the civilian populace, they have also left a legacy far greater than their military and economic impacts at the time, a legacy rife with stories of invasion and fifth columnist activity in both the United States and Australia that have endured up to the present day. The Japanese submarine campaigns against both countries are noteworthy as historical 'what could have been' scenarios, had the Japanese been more committed in taking the Pacific war to the American and Australian home fronts as they rode high following their conquests of 1941–42.

The story of Japan's emergence as the greatest Asian aggressor in history began with US Navy Commodore Matthew Perry's 'Black Ships' flotilla dropping anchor in Tokyo Bay in 1853, and only ended with the annihilation of the cities of Hiroshima and Nagasaki in 1945. Japan's journey was incredible, from an insular, feudal island nation ruled by a militarist warrior clique drawn from the *samurai* class headed by the *shogun*, to becoming the first Asian country to successfully challenge the regional hegemony of the Western Powers (led by Britain, France and the United States). From 1868, and the restoration of Emperor Meiji as head of state, alongside the creation of a modern democratic governmental system and military and naval establishment, the Japanese were anxious to prevent their country from becoming another China. Since the time of the First Opium War in 1841–42, Britain and the other Western Powers had come to dominate the weak Qing Dynasty of China. Millions of Chinese had become hooked on opium imported from Bengal in British India, and in return the white traders had made huge profits from this and every other form of trade with China. On each occasion that the ruling Qing Dynasty had attempted to control the spread of opium addiction and the activities of the 'foreign devils' inside the Celestial Empire, the Western nations had threatened the Chinese with punitive military expeditions. Each time the Imperial Court had backed down, and granted what the foreigners had asked for, namely complete control of China's foreign trade, and treaty ports such as Shanghai through which to regulate that trade, free of any legal restrictions under Manchu Chinese law. The Japanese observed this process and they quickly determined that Japan would not end up in a similar position to China, prostrated before the power and influence of Western trade interests. Unlike in China, the new Meiji government poured capital into new companies, such as Mitsui and Mitsubishi, building a strong economy that remained in the hands of the Japanese. In 1894 Japan was strong enough to begin looking overseas for territory to conquer, and colonies to possess in order that she might ape the European powers that dominated Asia. Japan picked a fight with, of all countries, China, which although the country's central government was weak and vacillating when faced with outside threats, nonetheless possessed a modern, British-constructed fleet, and a huge standing army. Most Westerners assumed that the upstart Japanese would be rudely defeated, but to widespread surprise it was the Chinese who were to lose the contest, firstly witnessing half of their fleet being sent to the bottom by the also largely British-built warships of the Imperial Japanese Navy at a battle at the mouth of the Yalu River in August 1894. The Japanese destroyed the remainder of China's fleet in August 1895 at a battle opposite the Chinese city of Wei Hai Wei (now Weihai). The Japanese demanded and received from China the island of Formosa (Taiwan), the Korean peninsula and the Pescadores.

In 1904 Japan shocked the entire world, and sent a shiver of fear running down the spines of the white governors and taipans of Asia when she engaged herself in war with Czarist Russia, which was considered to have one of the most up-to-date naval fleets in the world, and won. In 1904, the mighty Russian Baltic Fleet steamed halfway around the world intent on teaching the Japanese a severe lesson, only to be completely torn apart by Admiral Togo's British trained officers and men at the Battle of Tsushima. Although witness to heavy fighting on land, the Japanese also overcame and captured Russia's warm-water base in China, Port Arthur (now Lushun), in 1905. As Colin Smith notes, the '...victory over Czarist Russia had demonstrated its [Japan's] success in marrying western technology to the spirit of the samurai.'[2] The world was shocked because an Asian power, until then considered inferior in every way, had defeated a supposedly superior white nation, and such a result was unprecedented. It was also noted that although Britain's Royal Navy had been the force that had most directly influenced and moulded the Imperial Japanese Navy, the British had been used solely for their technology and the Japanese had not taken on the traditions and values of the Royal Navy. 'Royal Navy officers noticed that though their Japanese counterparts were eager to learn whatever they could about naval technology, strategy, and tactics, they had no interest in the Western civic values that went with them. Japan remained a nation driven by the samurai code of Bushido, the warrior values of its violent feudal past.'[3] This mindset was to make the Imperial Navy as savage and brutal in character and behaviour as any other part of the Japanese war machine, demonstrated in countless atrocities and acts of barbarity and cruelty committed by its officers and men throughout the course of the War of Aggression against China between 1937 and 1945, and the Pacific War of 1941 to 1945.

Just prior to the Russo-Japanese War the Imperial Navy had taken delivery of its first submarines from the United States, five Holland Class vessels. Although not destined to play a part in the war as the conflict ended before they could be deployed, these vessels became the nucleus of the future Japanese submarine force, joined shortly afterwards by two home-built examples. Japan had emerged from the war with Russia as a major sea power, and a possible future threat to the hegemony of Britain and the United States over the region's oceans. The Japanese worked closely with Britain in the design of some of her pre-First World War submarines, often in association with Vickers in the north of England. Japan, who was an ally of Britain and the United States during the First World War, benefited technologically from the German surrender in 1918. Seven former U-boats (all of them subsequently scrapped) were transferred to the Imperial Japanese Navy in 1919,[4] and sent to the giant Yokosuka Naval Base, located south of Tokyo. Alongside working examples of German submarine technology, Japan spent lavish sums of money attracting former U-boat officers, designers and technicians to work for the navy and large Japanese firms. The unequalled expertise of these Germans set alarm bells ringing throughout the intelligence organizations of the recently victorious Allied powers. By 1920 there were over 800 Germans formerly associated with U-boats as either submarine skippers and officers or designers and engineers working for the Japanese. American Military Intelligence noted that 'Engineers and ex-U-boat officers were most sought after, commanding the highest salaries,'[5] and of these 800, most were employed by Kawasaki, later to figure as a major submarine manufacturer in its own right.

As the Western Powers grew increasingly concerned about Japan's increasing naval strength they convened conferences in London in 1921 and Washington, DC and London in 1930. These meetings and the agreements that emerged from them limited the size of Japan's surface fleet so that Japan was unable to tip the balance of power in the Far East in her favour by outnumbering and outgunning the British and Americans. Around the time Britain and the United States first began to take steps to place serious limitations on the size and potency of the Japanese fleet, both the Japanese and US Navies had begun developing 'the strategic thesis of their fleets crossing an ocean for a major duel of capital ships. The concept had been articulated earlier in the widely read writings of American naval strategist Alfred Thayer Mahan.'[6] The United States understood that in order for their Pacific-based fleet to sortie westwards to any great range from the west coast it would have been necessary to have in place a series of forward bases. To this end the Americans began building up Pearl Harbor in Hawaii, Cavite in the Philippines and the island of Guam into superb naval bases allowing most of the fleet to be stationed well in advance of the American mainland. The Japanese watched these movements with great interest and decided that although their own surface fleet was strong, they were not as strong as the Americans. They decided that submarines would fill the gap in the strength of their battle fleet, and so design and construction began of huge, long-range submarines able to sally forth and attack the American fleet as it began its move westward. The submarines would serve two important purposes in countering the numerical superiority of the Americans by, firstly, slowly wearing down the enemy's strength to a size comparable with the Imperial battle fleet, which could meet it on more equal terms, and, secondly, it was envisioned that the submarines would act as an unseen reconnaissance screen giving the Japanese forewarning of American fleet movements.

The 1930 London Naval Conference was a disaster for the Japanese, because the terms of the agreement could have eroded Japan's submarine force, thereby leaving them hamstrung in any future efforts to stop an American advance westwards across the Pacific. However, the Washington Treaty, unbelievably, forced the British to reduce the size of their fleet to achieve parity with the Americans, Britain losing her hard won pre-eminence over the world's oceans held for over 200 years as inter-war economics encouraged government penny-pinching over the size and strength of the navy. However, both the London and Washington naval agreements failed to address properly the issue of submarine forces, and this oversight allowed the Japanese to concentrate a great effort on attempting to match, and better technologically, Britain and the United States in building up her submarine fleet. Much of the subsequent construction programme took place in great secrecy, in a similar way to German U-boat developments that were made in contravention of the 1919 Treaty of Versailles. Both fleet submarines and midget vessels were developed during the early 1930s, in the full expectation that these machines would see active service in the not-too-distant future as Japan convulsed internally between forces for Imperial expansion and those of democracy and friendship towards the West. In 1934 the Japanese government felt secure and strong enough to ignore the naval restrictions imposed on her in 1930, the Japanese arguing that such restrictions were unfair and Japan would have had difficulty in defending itself if it was to abide by the American and British instigated naval reductions. Although the Japanese were drawn back to the conference table in 1935, Japan took umbrage at what it perceived as the bullying attitude of the British and Americans towards her and withdrew the next year. Japan was by this stage already on the warpath, having flexed her military muscles in China several years before, and almost in the terminal grip of the militarists. After 1936 the Imperial Navy's fleet would grow steadily as the country began a massive warship construction programme that would culminate in the two biggest battleships ever built,

Musashi and *Yamato*, as well as a strong aircraft carrier force and submarine service.

In 1931, the riches afforded to Japanese industry and the military build-up then underway turned Japanese eyes covetously upon the northern Chinese province of Manchuria. Japanese militarists decided to engineer a confrontation with China. Manchuria was seized and renamed Manchukuo, and Japanese prime ministers who attempted to curb the ambitions of the militarists were routinely assassinated as the army and navy vied for power in Tokyo. The army prevailed and launched a full-scale war against China in 1937. The Chinese managed to resist sufficiently to prevent the Japanese achieving an easy, or swift, victory, although by 1938 most of eastern and southern China was under a brutal Japanese occupation in a war that was to last until 1945. The Japanese also courted an alliance with the world's other two aggressor nations, Hitler's Germany and Mussolini's Italy, making plans to divide up the world between themselves once the threats of the Soviet Union, Great Britain and the United States had been dealt with. In the event, Japan backed away from a war with the Soviet Union, later signing a non-aggression pact with Stalin, and the Japanese government monitored events in Europe carefully as Hitler began his *Blitzkrieg* campaign against the West. With the fall of France in June 1940, many of the colonies in the Far East, including French Indo-China and the Netherlands East Indies looked vulnerable. The British had also begun to appear militarily much weakened in the Far East, as the best naval units and most of the modern air force were withdrawn to fight the Germans and Italians in the Mediterranean and Middle East. The only real fly in the Japanese expansionist ointment was the unknowable reaction of the United States to any Japanese takeover of south-east Asia. The US Pacific Fleet, based at Pearl Harbor, Hawaii, was enormously powerful and would have to be neutralized by the Japanese concurrent with any operations to conquer the European colonies of Asia. A plan was drawn up for the commander of the Japanese Combined Fleets, Admiral Isoroku Yamamoto, in January 1941, outlining how the American threat could be removed from the equation. As Lord Russell notes, 'A surprise air attack was to be made by a special task force and was to be carried out while the two countries were still at peace. Were the attack successful, it was most likely that Japan would be able to occupy all her objectives in the Pacific and Indian Oceans before the United States could recover sufficiently from the blow to mount a counter-attack.'[7] Simultaneously, army and naval forces were to attack and occupy British Malaya and southern Thailand with the objective of capturing the modern naval base at Singapore. Other Japanese forces were to conquer the British colonies of Burma and Hong Kong, the Netherlands East Indies (now Indonesia), the Philippines, the International Settlement in Shanghai (which up to then had been regarded as neutral territory by Japanese forces occupying the rest of the city), and the Solomon and Central Pacific Islands. The Japanese had also been aware of the United States established strategy for any war that opened in the Pacific, the general naval advance westwards then known as 'Plan Orange'. Orange envisioned that the US Pacific Fleet would advance directly from Hawaii to relieve that other strategic outpost of America, the Philippines. Therefore, in Japanese naval minds since the 1930s there had been the conclusion that if the United States moved to prevent Japanese expansion into south-east Asia and the Pacific, there would inevitably be a major naval showdown somewhere in the Western Pacific, as the Japanese Combined Fleet collided with the US Pacific Fleet. When Japan signed up to the 1930 Washington Naval Treaty, the agreed capital ship ratio had been 5:5:3, Great Britain, the United States and Japan respectively. Therefore, the Royal Navy and most especially the US Pacific Fleet would outnumber and outgun the Imperial Fleet's surface vessels. Of course, by 1941, Britain's naval commitments in Europe and the Mediterranean had all but removed the Royal Navy from fending off any aggressive Japanese moves against her Asian colonies. As we have seen, for this reason, a determined effort was made by Japan to build up its submarine fleet to offset the imbalance created by the agreed warship ratio. In fact, submarines were going to have to play the role of the cruisers and destroyers Japan was forbidden to add to her fleet by the terms of the Washington Treaty, and this made the Japanese design and built a range of world-beating submarines far superior at the time to anything then in service with other navies, including the German Navy's U-boat Service. In the Japanese naval mind the Combined Fleet was designed to meet the US Pacific Fleet in one gigantic battle on a scale with the Japanese clash with Russia at Tsushima in 1904. It was therefore imperative that submarines be designed that were capable of engaging enemy warships, instead of only interdicting unarmed commercial traffic, and the idea remained current of removing some of the numerical advantage of the enemy before both fleets clashed. Of course, the eventual plan to attack the US Pacific Fleet in harbour made this plan largely redundant, the submarines designed to counter 'Plan Orange' had already been constructed and entered service by 1941, and Japanese submarine developments continued to produce extraordinary vessels throughout most of the rest of the war.

The very size of the Pacific Ocean meant that Japanese submarines, if they were to cooperate with the main fleet, would have to be big, with an extensive range, and capable of high surface speeds. Long-range fleet submarines, such as those that operated off Pearl Harbor and the American west coast between December 1941 and mid-1942, were very large, and capable of cruises approaching 20,000 nautical miles lasting a third of a year. It was only as the world entered the nuclear age after the Second World War that submarines began to outsize wartime Japanese models. Other innovations included speed, and although many Japanese submarines were huge, they were also swift, as they were required to stay close to the surface fleet acting in the role of cruisers. The Japanese did not ever possess a massive submarine fleet in terms of numbers of boats, but in terms of quality they were in advance of many comparable nations. The Germans fielded 1,171 U-boats during the entire period of the Second World War, but very few of their designs matched or surpassed Japanese long-range I-boats. Of 174 submarines employed by the Japanese during the Second World War (111 of which were built during the conflict), 110 were capable of submerged top speeds of 16 knots, and four of these could exceed an incredible 19 knots. This compares favourably with the most technologically advanced submarine type produced by any of the combatant nations during the Second World War, the German Type XXI electro-boat, which was capable of a top submerged speed of 17.5 knots (and only one of these advanced boats actually conducted a war patrol before the German surrender in May 1945).

In December 1941 the Imperial Navy had available sixty-three operational submarines for immediate deployment on operations, a total that included forty-eight of the large I-boats. A further twenty-nine submarines were under construction in Japan, and were scheduled for completion in 1942–43. Their main opponent, the US Navy, had a total of 111 submarines in commission, with another seventy-three under construction. However, only fifty-one boats were assigned to the Asiatic and Pacific Fleets. The British no longer deployed a single submarine in the Pacific, or at any of its naval bases throughout south-east Asia, while the Netherlands had eleven boats assigned to her Asian colonies.[8] Most Japanese submarines, certainly most of the powerful long-range I-boats were under the control of 6th Fleet. Vice-Admiral Mitsumi Shimizu would command this potent force consisting of the 1st, 2nd and 3rd Submarine Squadrons (each under a rear-admiral) from a forward base established soon after hostilities commenced at Kwajalein in the Marshall Islands. Shimizu's flagship was the light cruiser *Katori*. Each submarine squadron was itself sub-divided into several divisions, each under the command of a sea-going captain, with individual submarines usually skippered by a lieutenant-commander. Combined Fleet Headquarters retained control over the 4th and 5th Submarine Squadrons, used to support to invasions of the Philippines and Malaya, with the 6th Squadron going to the 3rd Fleet (Blockade & Transport) also in support of the same amphibious operations. The 7th Squadron was under the operational control of 4th Fleet, and with its generally obsolescent vessels was tasked with protecting the Home Islands and the Mandated Islands under pre-war Japanese control in the Pacific. Finally, the Kure Naval District operated several second-line submarines that were considered unsuitable for open sea operations, and these vessels were used for crew training and homeland defence (see Appendix 1 for a complete breakdown of Japanese submarine organization at the beginning of the war.)

Fifty-two Japanese submarines displaced in excess of 3,000 tons, and at the war's end they had even produced underwater aircraft carriers, the I-400-class, with a displacement exceeding 5,000 tons when submerged, and a length of over 400 feet. Forty-one of Japan's Second World War submarines could carry aircraft, making the Imperial Navy the only fleet on earth capable of this innovation.[9]

Another innovation was in the field of torpedoes, and Japan was the world's leader in their design. The famous Type 95 21-inch calibre torpedo, also known as the 'Long Lance', had the longest range of any torpedo then in existence, a mighty 12,000 metres at a speed of 45 knots. The 23-foot 5-inch weapon could deliver a warhead considerably more powerful than the best American torpedo, initially 893-pounds of TNT and hexanitrodiphenylamine, later increased to 1,080-pounds. What was truly revolutionary about the Long Lance was its propulsion system, another massive technological leap forward. The Type 95 burned oxygen in turn to ignite kerosene, instead of the more conventional compressed air and alcohol used by every other navy in the world. This meant that the Long Lance multiplied its range over Allied torpedoes, and the propulsion system drastically reduced any telltale wake of bubbles in the water that would allow enemy ships to take evasive action. A simple, yet highly reliable, contact exploder triggered the massive warhead, so the Japanese were not plagued as regularly by the kinds of torpedo failures suffered by German U-boats and American submarines in the earlier stages of the war.[10]

With advantages in submarine technology and torpedoes, innovations in submarine-mounted aircraft and massive patrol ranges, it is perhaps surprising that the Japanese were not more successful at sea during the course of the war. During the Pacific War's early stages it was not the technology that was to fail Japan, but the strategic and tactical use of that technology against the Allies. Because of the entrenched belief in a large battle in the Western Pacific in reaction to the American's 'Plan Orange', submarines were firmly tied to fleet cooperation, and not given over to commerce raiding as practiced by the larger German U-boat Service with such devastating results for Britain's merchant marine. As we shall see, the operations discussed in this book marked Japan's very quixotic attempts to interdict commerce and conduct fleet actions using submarines, and priority was always given to the fleet. Between 1939 and 1945 German U-boats sank 2,840 merchant ships, while Japanese submarines between the end of 1941 and 1945 sank 184. The difference in focus is clearly marked when one considers how potent a force the Japanese submarine fleet was, how devastating its weapons had the potential to be, and how well trained and above all determined were its men.

Even as the plans were being finalized for the series of attacks the Japanese desired to make on the colonial powers and the United States in December 1941, elements in the Imperial Navy still opposed opening a second war front before the army had successfully overcome resistance in China. Japan's last senior dissenting voice to the proposed plan was Prince Konoye, the Prime Minister, and he was forced to resign in the face of intense pressure from the army on 18 October. His replacement sealed the fate of Japan and demonstrated to the world that Japan had become to all intents and purposes a military dictatorship. Serving army officer General Hideki Tojo succeeded to the post of Prime Pinister, and final plans for the decimation of the US Pacific Fleet were made on 1 November. On the 5 November 1941 Admiral Isoroku Yamamoto, commander of the Combined Fleet, issued the operational orders green lighting the air assault on Pearl Harbor. The purpose of the operation was to 'damage U.S. forces sufficiently to keep them temporarily on the defensive and to prevent the American battle fleet from intervening with the Japanese southern advance'.[11] The submarine part of the Combined Fleet attack on Pearl Harbor would consist of three elements, conducting three overall mission objectives. Firstly, the submarines would precede the main aircraft carrier fleet steaming towards Hawaii. As outlined in Admiral Yamamoto's Combined Fleet Operations Order[12] issued to the Japanese 6th Fleet (Submarines), the submarines were ordered to 'Make reconnaissance of American Fleet in Hawaii and west coast areas and, by surprise attacks on shipping, destroy lines of communications'.[13] The three vessels of the 2nd Submarine Division were allocated as a Patrol Unit to conduct the reconnaissance, with the *I-19* acting as flagship, assisted by the *I-21* and *I-23*. If the submarines sighted any enemy warships they were to track them, but were forbidden from launching any attacks until the air strike was under way. Following the air strikes, the submarines were to linger around the entrance to Pearl Harbor, and the area of ocean between Hawaii and the west coast and attack any American warships attempting to flee the carnage at Pearl Harbor. They were to also prevent the Americans from bringing reinforcements up to Hawaii from the mainland to reinforce the hopefully severely damaged Pacific Fleet. An attack was also to be made by midget submarines on Pearl Harbor slightly before the main air strike arrived aimed at sinking enemy warships found at anchor. In tactical command of all submarine forces involved in the Pearl Harbor operation was Rear-Admiral Tsutomu Sato aboard his flagship, the submarine *I-9*. His forces were derived from the 1st Submarine Squadron, and the Special Attack Force (midget submarines), subdivided into three separate units. The Carrier Strike Force would consist of two waves of torpedo and high-altitude naval bombers escorted by Zero fighters, flying from six aircraft carriers led by the *Akagi*, flagship of the Strike Force commander, Admiral Nagumo. The submarines of Vice-Admiral Mitsumi Shimizu's 6th Fleet formed part of the Advance Expeditionary Force, but Admiral Sato retained tactical command at sea of the vessels involved in the operation. Shimizu's force, which comprised all of 1st, 2nd and 3rd Submarine Squadrons, consisted of seventeen I-class submarines[14] and five Type-A midgets. Operations Order No. 1 further elucidated upon the four functions the submarines of the Advance Expeditionary Force were to perform during the Pearl Harbor operation. Firstly, until X-day (7 December 1941) minus 3 days some of Shimizu's submarines were to conduct covert reconnaissance of the Aleutian Islands, Fiji and Samoa, and were to report on any strong American naval forces discovered to be thereabouts. Secondly, one element was assigned to patrol the route of the Striking Force, as it made its way across the Pacific. It was vital to protect the main force from enemy detection so the air strikes would come as a complete surprise. Thirdly, until X-day minus 5 the remaining submarines of the 6th Fleet were to surround Hawaii at extreme range while several boats approached the islands to reconnoitre. Fourthly, on X-day itself, submarines in the area were to 'observe and attack the American fleet in the Hawaii area; make a surprise attack on the channel leading into Pearl Harbor [the job of the five midget submarines] and attempt to close it; if the enemy moves out to fight, he will be pursued and attacked.'[15]

In the meantime, to keep the Americans guessing as to Japan's next move, diplomatic channels were kept open, culminating with Japanese Ambassador Nomura presenting Secretary of State Cordell Hull with a set of unacceptable demands in Washington DC on 26 November, the same day the massive Japanese carrier taskforce set sail from the Home Islands on a course for Hawaii.

The stage was thus set for one of history's most memorable attacks, an attack largely remembered today not only for its treachery and surprise, but primarily for its innovative use of carrier aircraft against warships. One element of the Pearl Harbor attack that has often been overlooked was the role of Japan's submarine service. The plan called for the Type-A midget submarines and their young crews to prove their worth and help Japan smash the power of the US fleet in a decisive aerial and submarine onslaught. Their success or failure to neutralize the American battle fleet on 7 December would have far reaching consequences for the entire Japanese strategic plan, and for the survival and prosperity of the empire Japan was about to carve out for itself in south-east Asia.

Notes

1. The final shots fired in anger on the American mainland between United States and British forces occurred at New Orleans, Louisiana in 1815, after the War of 1812 had been concluded. Due to the poor state of communications of the period news of a treaty agreement ending the war in 1814 was late reaching the respective generals.
2. Colin Smith, *Singapore Burning: Heroism and Surrender in World War II*, (London: Viking), 2005, p.59
3. Arthur Herman, *To Rule the Waves: How the British Navy Shaped the Modern World*, (London: Hodder & Stoughton), 2005, p.522
4. David Miller, *U-Boats: History, Development and Equipment 1914–1945*, (London: Conway Maritime Press), 2000, p.14
5. Carl Boyd & Akira Yoshida, *The Japanese Submarine Force and World War II*, (Shrewsbury: Airlife Publishing Ltd.), 1996, p.14
6. Norman Polmar & Dorr B. Carpenter, *Submarines of the Imperial Japanese Navy 1904–1945*, (London: Conway Maritime Press), 1986, p.1
7. Lord Russell of Liverpool, *The Knights of Bushido: A Short History of Japanese War Crimes*, (London: Greenhill Books), 2002, p.31
8. Norman Polmar & Dorr B. Carpenter, op. cit.
9. Data derived from Bob Hackett and Sander Kingsepp's website: http://www.combinedfleet.com/sensuikan.htm, from essay *Japan's Submarine Fleet*
10. ibid. essay *Japanese Torpedoes*
11. Norman Polmar & Dorr B. Carpenter, op. cit., p.55

12. Combined Fleet Telegraphic Operations Order No. 021730
13. *Japanese Monograph No. 97, Pearl Harbor Operations: General Outline of Orders and Plans*, (Washington DC: Office of the Chief of Military History, Department of the Army), 1953, p.28
14. *I-1,I-2, I-3, I-4, I-5, I-6, I-7, I-16, I-17, I-18, I-20, I-22, I-23, I-24, I-68, I-69, I-74*
15. *Report of the Joint Committee on the Investigation of the Pearl Harbor attack, Congress of the United States*, (Washington DC: Government Printing Office), 1946, p.63

Chapter 2

Steel Coffins: 7 December 1941

In the first six to twelve months of a war with the United States and Great Britain I will run wild and win victory upon victory. But then, if the war continues after that, I have no expectation of success.

Admiral Isoroku Yamamoto before the Pearl Harbor operation, 1941

On 28 November 1941 the Japanese First Special Attack Flotilla, consisting of the submarines *I-16, I-18, I-20, I-22* and *I-24*, each carrying a single Type-A midget submarine clamped to the deck abaft the conning tower, began their journeys across the north Pacific to Hawaii. Aboard the *I-22* was Captain Hanku Sasaki, commanding the flotilla, and he had issued orders that the submarines were to maintain a twenty-mile gap between one another as they journeyed across the ocean. Once out of Japanese territorial waters each submarine skipper informed the crew of their mission, and the purpose of the strange cargo they were hauling. Aboard the *I-22*, the skipper, Commander Kiyoi Ageta, declared to the assembled complement packed into the control room and the corridors leading away fore and aft: 'Our ship is sailing for Hawaii now. Our objective is to discharge the special-type storage tube [a reference to the classified Type-A] to attack Pearl Harbor.'[1] The leader of the midget submarines once the flotilla had launched from the mother ships was Lieutenant Naoji Iwasa who was also based aboard the *I-22*.

Captain Sasaki's plan of action for the five midget submarines constituting his Special Attack Force was simple. The midgets were to penetrate Pearl Harbor undetected and stay concealed inside the harbour until the main air assault began. Several options were then open to the midget submarine skippers. Firstly, once the first Japanese aircraft appeared overhead, they could immediately begin attacks on American warships inside the harbour. Secondly, the midget submarine commanders could wait for the lull between the first and second Japanese aerial waves, and attack then, creating an offensive bridge between the first two aerial assaults. Thirdly, the midget submarines could continue to remain concealed throughout the duration of the carrier plane assaults, only to emerge from the depths with the coming of darkness, and as the Americans began cleaning up launch their attacks by travelling anti-clockwise around Ford Island. Regardless of which plan the submarine skippers activated, their aim was to expend their torpedoes and then depart Pearl Harbor and make for the rendezvous point with the mother submarines at Lanai Island and recovery. Of course, these plans hinged on any of the five Type-As actually penetrating the entrance to Pearl Harbor undetected.

The weapons, which the First Flotilla was to launch against Pearl Harbor hours before the arrival of the main aerial attack force, were intriguing creations reflecting Japanese ingenuity and the advance of naval warfare. The vessels were not small, each Type-A midget submarine measuring 78.5 feet in length and weighing forty-six tons. A two-man crew consisted of a junior officer who commanded the boat and an enlisted man who acted primarily as helmsman. The Type-A could managed 19 knots submerged, and had a potential maximum range of 100 miles if running on the surface at a conservative 2 knots. The midget would approach its target surfaced until diving for the final attack run. The role of the junior officer midget commander was to give helm orders and operate the submarine's periscope. The commander decided the submarine's course, speed and depth, and, of course, targets, and transmitted these orders to the petty officer helmsman. The petty officer was charged primarily with control of the helm, and he was required to keep his hands on the wheel for the duration of the mission as the midget was extremely sensitive and the helmsman could easily lose control of the vessel. The petty officer was also required to dive and surface the boat by pulling and turning an assortment of valves that operated the midget's ballast tanks. Finally, when given the order by the commander, he was charged with firing the two 17 feet long 18-inch torpedoes loaded in the midgets two 'under and over' tubes in the bow. Each torpedo was packed with 300 pounds of TNT. The single greatest challenge faced by the midget crews, apart from heat exhaustion and being unable to stand up inside the vessel for hours on end, was maintaining the submarine's balance, the Type-A being renowned for its instability at sea.[2]

The 'mother' submarines that would transport the midgets to the waters around Hawaii were all of the Type-C1-class. Five of these vessels were completed in 1940 and 1941 respectively,[3] and they were dedicated midget submarine transports. As well as the Pearl Harbor operation, the Type-C1 submarines *I-16* and *I-20* launched their midgets outside of the Royal Navy's base at Diego Suarez in Madagascar on the night of 30 May 1942. Although neither the crews or the midget submarines themselves returned to the 'mother' ships they did manage to damage the old British battleship HMS *Ramillies*, and to sink the tanker *British Loyalty* inside the anchorage. The very next night, 31 May, thousands of miles to the east, the *I-22* and *I-24* (along with other Japanese submarines) launched their midgets in an attempt to penetrate Sydney harbour in Australia (related in Chapter 5).

In November 1942 the *I-16, I-20* and *I-24* all launched midgets off Guadalcanal, but the damage inflicted to a single American transport was a heavy price to pay for the loss of all of the Type-A midgets that participated in the operation.

When fully loaded the 358.5 feet long Type-C1 submarine weighed in at 3,561 tons, and was powered by twin diesel engines generating 12,400 horsepower. This meant that the submarine could reach 23.5 knots on the surface, and an equally impressive 8 knots when running submerged on 2,000 horsepower electric motors. At a fuel-conserving 16 knots a surfaced Type C1 could sail 14,000 nautical miles without refuelling. However, the boats' trim characteristics were shot to pieces by each having a forty-six ton midget submarine armed with two torpedoes secured to their decks. The submarines travelled submerged by day to avoid aerial detection, coming to the surface at night to charge their batteries. Heavy winter seas constantly washed over the submarines' decks as the maintenance crews charged with taking care of the midgets clambered and skidded about. The crewmen had to tie themselves to the submarines with lifelines, and many were washed overboard by the waves, only to climb back onto the decks bruised, exhausted and coughing up seawater. Onboard the *I-24* one of the midget's torpedoes was damaged when the mother ship submerged, and it took the crew a full night in foul weather to fit a new torpedo, manhandling the steel fish up from inside the cluttered and cramped interior of the *I-24* and into the midget.

Unlike the Type-B1 submarine utilized by the Japanese in patrolling the American west coast in 1941–42, the Type-C1 was not fitted with a reconnaissance aircraft. Armed with a total of twenty torpedoes, eight torpedo tubes were arranged in the bow, served via two separate torpedo rooms located one above the other. The type also mounted a 140mm (5.5-inch) deck-gun, and a rather inadequate single .50 cal. machine gun for anti-aircraft defence. One hundred and one men were required to crew each Type-C1 submarine, a huge complement for a submarine of the era and once again not matched or surpassed until the nuclear age.

As the *I-22* crept closer to Oahu, Sasaki watched the coastline intently, but little stirred ashore in the darkness. A few lights were visible and an occasional searchlight beam punched out into the night sky. Sasaki's confidence soared, and he began to believe that the boys of the Special Attack Force really would be successful and prove the value of their training and their innovative new equipment. As the five midget submarines and the ten hand-picked officers and seamen prepared to strike at the mighty American fleet resting at anchor, Sasaki had '...a feeling of confidence and a renewed hope that the attack would be successful'.[4] The *I-24*'s midget developed a further problem, this time a malfunctioning gyro-compass, a vital piece of equipment without which navigation would have been almost impossible. Ensign Kazuo Sakamaki, the midget's commander, and Petty Officer Second Class Kiyoshi Inagaki, the crewman, worked feverishly to correct the problem and insisted that their mission should go ahead even if the compass was not fixed in time, demonstrating both their eagerness to complete a mission they had spent months training for, and a willingness to disregard their own lives in the process. Commander Hiroshi Hanabusa, skipper of the *I-24*, reluctantly agreed to this request, not overly keen to send men on one-way missions, because as an experienced seaman he knew full well that the chances of Sakamaki and Inagaki returning from the mission would be remote with such faulty equipment to contend with.

As the sun slowly set on Saturday, 6 December 1941, the five Japanese mother submarines had assumed their midget launch positions approximately eight miles south of the entrance to Pearl Harbor. The radio operators aboard were periodically picking up Hawaiian music from the shore that echoed eerily through the boats as men moved about making last minute adjustments to their equipment, and officers peered intently through periscopes at the darkened land before them. Slightly after midnight the *I-16* began the launch of Sub-Lieutenant Masaharu Yokoyama, aged twenty-two, and his midget. After the launch the *I-16* was to proceed to the second, and some would have argued even then, rather unrealistic stage, of the flotilla battle plan: to await the return of the midgets from their attacks on Pearl Harbor. The five big submarines would position themselves seven miles west of Lanai Island, which itself is eighty miles east of Pearl Harbor. There the plan called for them to wait for two days before departing the area. When (if) the midget submarines managed to locate a mother submarine at this location, the midget's crew was to be recovered and the Type-A then scuttled. Because the mother submarines would fan out off Lanai Island, more than one midget might rendezvous with the same submarine, so it was decided that recovery of the Type-As was impractical. The exhausted but hopefully victorious crews would have priority, as the equipment could be replaced. All of this was rather academic, as many officers and men aboard both the mother submarines and midgets knew, for the midget crews had already made their peace with God, and were prepared to sell their lives for the sake of the Emperor.

Yokoyama and his crewman, Petty Officer Second Class Sadamu Ueda, had already made their preparations for what they believed to be their final voyage. Should they be killed they would become 'War Gods', venerated at the Yasakuni Shrine in Tokyo. They could take satisfaction that if they died the Emperor himself would visit the shrine each year to pay his respects and pray for their souls. Religious rites had been conducted aboard the submarine, prayers said, and final farewell letters penned to their families back in Japan, the men enclosing locks of hair and fingernail clippings so that their families would have something physical to cremate should they perish. Both men had dressed in clean uniforms, as *Shinto* rites dictated, and with souls and bodies purified they had clambered up into their midget submarine from inside the *I-16*. The telephone link between the midget and the mother submarine was disconnected and at 12.42 a.m. on Sunday, 7 December, the midget lifted off under the water and departed for war.

Aboard the command submarine *I-22* Lieutenant Iwasa, leader of the midget submarine group once they had left the mother ships, and his crewmen, Petty Officer First Class Naokichi Sasaki, clambered aboard their vessel. Both men carried family swords strapped to their backs in white cloth sashes. Just before Iwasa disappeared up the ladder into the Type-A he briefly addressed the crew of the *I-22*. He was full of gratitude for their assistance in getting him and Sasaki to the target area: 'Our work begins now. Believing in divine help, we are about to depart to do our utmost to fulfil our final task so as not to betray your trust and expectation in us,' he said, adding, 'I pray for the future successful battles of *I-22*. Farewell.'[5] Iwasa bowed to the crew, who returned his salute, and then was sealed inside the midget. Grasping the inter-submarine telephone, Sasaki spoke to Iwasa for the final time before the midget departed. 'Congratulations in advance on your success', he said, 'I hope you will do your job well. Good luck!' Iwasa thanked his commanding officer for bringing all of them this far, and his final words indicated his acceptance of the nature of the coming mission when he said, 'I wish you [Sasaki] to look after my private affairs.'[6] With the final farewells said the midget was released into the open sea at 1.15 a.m. The *I-22*'s crew faced the direction the midget had sailed and saluted in silence. It was now a waiting game, waiting for news of a series of successful attacks made by the men they had come to know during the journey across the Pacific, and a period of waiting for their triumphant return, however remote that possibility appeared.

A similar scene to that being played out aboard the *I-22* had just concluded aboard the *I-18*, as Sub-Lieutenant Shigemi Furuno and Petty Officer First Class Shigenori Yokoyama lifted off and motored towards Pearl Harbor. Next to depart was Ensign Akira Hiro-o and Petty Officer Second Class Yoshio Katayama from the *I-20*. Aboard the *I-24*, the midget's defective gyro-compass was still not functioning properly, so Sakamaki determined to navigate towards Pearl Harbor at periscope depth instead, navigating by eye. It was a suicidal decision, but both men were determined not to be left behind kicking their heels while their comrades made history. They were the last midget to depart, and lifted off at 3.33 a.m. The loss of the gyro-compass was soon keenly felt by Sakamaki, as he vainly tried to hold the submarine on a course for the harbour by taking regular periscope readings, but the midget floundered about, taking a long time to edge towards his objective as the dawn fast approached. All of the midgets were supposed to penetrate the entrance to the harbour before daybreak, and be in position to time their attacks with those of the carrier task force aircraft. This became increasingly remote for Sakamaki and his submarine as the slow progress meant he would arrive at the entrance to Pearl Harbor after the other midgets, and the American base would be fully alert to a Japanese presence.

The first line of defence that the five Japanese midget submarines would encounter, and have to slip by unnoticed if they had a chance of penetrating the harbour, were three American minesweepers, the USS *Crossbill, Condor* and *Reedbird*. Their job was to patrol the harbour approaches, and a First World War-vintage destroyer located behind them supported them in this task. The USS *Ward* had been launched during the middle of 1918, though she had not seen any action during the earlier conflict. In fact, the *Ward* had never fired her guns in anger, and after the First World War the vessel had been mothballed and placed in reserve at San Diego until called up for service in early 1941. Commissioned back into service, and assigned to the US Pacific Fleet as a harbour defence and patrol vessel, she was placed under the command of thirty-five year old Lieutenant William Outerbridge. At 3.57 a.m. the *Condor* reported sighting what appeared to be a small submarine periscope about two miles outside of the harbour buoy, and the *Ward* motored over to assist in a thorough search. The *Ward* conducted a sonar search but turned up no contacts, and after ninety minutes gave up and returned to her original patrol sector.

The next line of defence designed to prevent unauthorized penetration of Pearl Harbor was an anti-submarine and boat net stretched across the harbour mouth. Sections of this net could be opened to permit the passage of vessels into and out of the harbour, and it was the job of the patrol vessels to monitor who was coming and going. Around 5 a.m. the patrol boats *Condor* and *Crossbill* headed into the harbour through a gate that was opened for them. The gate was left open as the USS *Antares*, a navy repair ship towing an empty steel barge, was expected to pass through shortly afterwards. Sub-Lieutenant Yokoyama, aboard the *I-16*'s midget, saw his chance and decided to follow the *Antares* through the gate, hopefully fooling the sentinels on watch. Lookouts aboard the *Ward* watched the *Antares* pass in front of their vessel as she made her way towards the gate. Something, however, caught their attention, for their appeared to be an object moving in the water between the repair ship and the barge. After some animated discussions aboard the *Ward*, it was concluded that the object was most probably a loose buoy. Pearl Harbor had received many submarine sightings over the past year, all of which had turned out to be false alarms, and no one was in the mood for jumping to conclusions just yet. The sun was up by now, and the officers and lookouts took up their binoculars and trained them on the object in the water for a closer look. The 'buoy' appeared to be travelling at about 5 knots, and no one knew of an inanimate navigational marker doing this before. Lieutenant Outerbridge faced a dilemma: perhaps the object was some kind of new secret weapon being developed by the US Navy, and if he fired on it the consequences for him could have been dire. However, he had not been informed by 14th Naval District to expect any such activity in his sector, and the object was, after all, inside the restricted zone. Having made up his mind to attack the object, Outerbridge ordered the guns manned and the men to battle stations. By now seamen aboard both the *Ward* and the *Antares* were reporting that the object looked much less like a buoy, and much more like a small submarine conning tower cutting the surface of the water like a shark's dorsal fin. A

Catalina flying boat circling overhead had also taken an interest in the object, and dropped some smoke bombs to mark its position for the warships.

At 6.45 a.m. the *Ward* opened fire, the first shot from its No. 1 gun sailing over the little conning tower to land in the sea beyond. At this point the midget submarine was seen to noticeably increase speed, the commander evidently attempting to charge the open gate in the net and get inside the harbour. Shot number two from the *Ward* decided the issue, however, as the round ploughed into the base of the conning tower, but did not explode. The midget immediately heeled over violently and started to sink. Outerbridge decided to make sure and passed alongside the foundering submarine, four depth charges rolling off the back of the destroyer. The detonations finished the Japanese submarine, and she disappeared rapidly into the disturbed sea. The *Ward* now signalled to shore a message for the attention of Rear-Admiral Claude C. Bloch, Commandant of the 14th Naval District, and responsible for the Pearl Harbor base and facilities: 'We have dropped depth charges upon sub operating in defensive area.' Theoretically, such a message should have set alarm bells ringing all over Pearl Harbor that something was amiss, but when the first message was received (a second followed a couple of minutes later) at the Harbor Control Post at 6.51 a.m., getting the signals sent up the chain of command quickly proved difficult. A twenty-minute delayed ensued while the messages were decoded and re-sent, and because it was very early on Sunday morning only skeleton crews were manning the communication equipment anyway. The duty officer in charge of the security of the anti-submarine and ship net guarding the harbour, Lieutenant Harold Kaminski, took it upon himself to try to get things moving regarding some sort of response to the *Ward*'s messages. He telephoned Admiral Bloch's chief-of-staff, Captain John B. Earle, and Kaminski also ordered the ready-duty destroyer, the USS *Monaghan*, to 'proceed immediately and contact the *Ward* in defensive in sea area'.[7] Captain Earle in turn telephoned Admiral Bloch, and the two senior officers discussed the reports, and concluded that it was probably just another false submarine sighting. With the *Monaghan* assisting the *Ward* the two vessels were more than capable of dealing with the situation. Earle told

Kaminski to inform the 6th Fleet's Operations Officer of the event, but to take no further action. Confusion reigned ashore, as the *Ward* now reported that she had intercepted a fishing sampan inside the security defence zone, and required a navy cutter to escort the vessel away from the vicinity. When Earle was informed he wondered why the *Ward* would go off intercepting sampans when she believed a submarine to be in the area, and concluded that the *Ward*'s crew had misidentified their earlier submarine contact. Therefore, it was just another false alarm.

The Japanese air armada of carrier aircraft, led by Commander Mitsuo Fuchida, was fast approaching Oahu. Another American destroyer, the USS *Chew*, reported to 14th Naval District that she had attacked and sunk a midget submarine outside the entrance to the harbour. The *Ward* continued depth-charging operations as American patrol vessels charged about seeing submarines everywhere. They were still busily engaged in this when the first Japanese aircraft passed overhead and roared down to bomb and strafe Ford Island, Battleship Row and Hickam Field US Army Air Corps base. The reports of submarine contacts were soon drowned out by the full-scale aerial assault being made on the naval base and vessels moored in the harbour. The *Ward* and the *Monaghan* sounded 'General Quarters' at 8 a.m., after a Japanese bomb landed close to the *Monaghan*. Anti-aircraft guns were hastily manned, the crews doing what they could to return fire against the Japanese planes knocking Pearl Harbor and the Pacific Fleet to pieces virtually at will.

By 8.14 a.m. the harbour patrol destroyers had commenced a steady anti-aircraft barrage directed against Commander Fuchida's carrier air group. The *Monaghan* was ordered to move down the harbour approach channel, and while making this journey she encountered the seaplane tender USS *Curtiss* at 8.53 a.m. Although a massive air battle raged overhead, the *Curtiss* was flying signal flags indicating that a submarine was threatening her. Crewmen aboard the destroyer watched as the *Curtiss* trained her guns on the water and opened fire at a floating object. The destroyer quickly identified the object as a small submarine before the craft slinked beneath the surface, reappearing at 8.40 a.m. This midget submarine was well within the harbour defences, cruising around off Ford Island in the centre of the harbour. The midget had been able to penetrate so deeply into Pearl Harbor because, as related earlier, a gate had been left open from 5 a.m. that morning at the entrance to allow the USS *Antares* to enter. It had remained open while the destroyer USS *Ward* had attacked and sunk a midget submarine by the harbour entrance, and no one had subsequently closed the boom and net as Pearl Harbor came under sustained and heavy air attack that morning. The midget that was lurking off Ford Island shot a single torpedo that sailed past the *Curtiss*, narrowly missing the light cruiser USS *Rayleigh*, before running into the land opposite Pearl City and exploding.

The *Monaghan* now attempted to deal with the midget, firing a single 5-inch shell at the small conning tower from her main gun, but the midget turned about and shot its final torpedo at the destroyer. The Japanese torpedo shot past the *Monaghan* and blew up when it struck land at Ford Island. Lieutenant-Commander W. P. Burford, captain of the *Monaghan*, decided upon a drastic course of action at this point. He ordered the engine room to give him full speed, and then pointed the destroyer's bows at the little submarine and set to ram it. After a few seconds the destroyer struck the midget, which was dragged along the length of the *Monaghan* before it passed by. A quick-thinking torpedoman stationed in the destroyer's stern watched the midget submarine trail along the side of his ship, and quickly fused a depth charge that he dropped overboard alongside the midget. Burford ordered another depth charge dropped, but then the *Monaghan* ran aground onto a submerged mud bank. The two depth charges exploded, and great geysers of seawater, black with oil, shot high into the air marking the destruction of the Japanese submarine. The *Monaghan* extricated herself from the mud. All the time this little action was occurring Japanese air attacks continued all around the Americans, but the *Monaghan* and her crew were unharmed.

The Japanese submariners continued in their efforts to press home attacks on the US fleet. At 9.50 a.m. the destroyer USS *Blue* obtained a contact with a suspected submarine outside the harbour. The *Blue* laid a pattern of depth charges and reported the probable destruction of the enemy vessel. Attempting to exit the carnage that was Pearl Harbor that morning, the light cruiser

USS *St. Louis* dodged two torpedoes running towards her before they exploded. A small submarine conning tower was seen, and the cruiser engaged the target with her main batteries, claiming to have scored hits.

The *I-24*'s temperamental Type-A, whose defective gyrocompass had almost cost Ensign Sakamaki his place on the mission, was now the only midget still operational. Sakamaki's boat, however, had been extensively damaged by the depth charge barrages laid at the harbour entrance. The midget's steering gear was almost gone, and the batteries were cracked and leeching noxious fumes into the crew compartment as Sakamaki and Petty Officer Inagaki struggled to nurse their vessel towards the harbour entrance channel, and its open gate. Both men were buoyed up immensely when Sakamaki viewed through the periscope the huge columns of black smoke rising from Pearl Harbor, indicating the success of the aerial assault. Sakamaki was determined that he would add to the destruction with his two torpedoes, never considering abandoning his mission and attempting to rendezvous with the mother submarines. At 8.15 a.m. Sakamaki surfaced the boat to attempt to locate the harbour entrance and a potential target through his periscope, only to have the American destroyer USS *Helm* loom large in the lens as the ship raced for the open sea. The destroyer clearly discerned the midget submarine limping towards the harbour entrance. As the two vessels converged, the Japanese submarine ground onto a submerged reef, exposing herself completely to the *Helm*'s guns. But, although the destroyer blazed away no hits were made, and gingerly, Sakamaki was able to get the Type-A off the reef and submerged. Once beneath the waves the two Japanese sailors assessed their situation. The air inside the submarine was becoming unbearable, and the men were in danger of being overcome by the battery fumes. The defective steering meant the Type-A wallowed around uncontrollably, making directed movement or assuming a firing position almost impossible. One of the torpedo tubes had also become inoperable as a result of striking the reef, so Sakamaki decided to use his entire vessel as one giant torpedo and ram the next American warship they encountered. This would result in their deaths, but both men were fully committed to such an end. For the rest of the morning

Sakamaki vainly tried to obtain some measure of control over the submarine, but another grounding on a reef knocked out the second torpedo tube. The midget was now adrift, with the crew swimming in and out of consciousness in the thick air inside the submarine, as they attempted to reach Lanai Island and the mother ships waiting there. Sakamaki opened the submarines hatch to air the crew compartment, before falling asleep again, and for the rest of the night of the 7–8 December the submarine drifted about, hatch open, crew asleep until further efforts were made to use the engine to get them to Lanai. The engine barely worked, and the attempt was abandoned, for without a compass they also had no idea where they were, and which direction salvation lay. At some point on the early morning of 8 December the midget submarine ran aground for the final time on a reef some way off a deserted beach. Sakamaki ordered the vessel abandoned, and the two Japanese plunged into the heavy sea and attempted to swim for the shore. Unfortunately, Petty Officer Inagaki was lost in the waves and drowned, while Sakamaki washed up exhausted but alive on Waimanalo Beach, close to a devastated Bellow's Field Army Air Corps base. Sakamaki came ashore virtually into the arms of a patrol of American soldiers from the 298th Infantry Regiment and was taken prisoner. Sakamaki was the first Japanese serviceman taken prisoner during the Second World War, and the young naval officer was stricken with humiliation and shame. It was to prove an intelligence coup for the Americans, and they hoped to discover from Sakamaki more about the strange little submarines that had so boldly attacked the anchorage.

The First Special Attack Flotilla's assault on Pearl Harbor was an abject failure. All of the Type-As were destroyed during the operation, and not a single torpedo fired by the midgets struck a single American ship. Of the ten sailors who crewed the vessels, only Ensign Sakamaki survived the ordeal. However, the men who undertook the mission had not really thought much of their chances of coming back alive. The Imperial Japanese Navy honoured the memories of the nine dead men, and they were elevated to the level of war-gods, and posthumously promoted. Lieutenant Iwasa, the leader of the First Special Attack Flotilla was promoted to commander. Yokoyama and Furuno were advanced to lieutenant-commanders, and Ensign Hiro-o was made a lieutenant. Petty Officer First Class Yokoyama and Sasaki were commissioned with the rank of special ensign, while Petty Officer Second Class Ueda, Katayama and Inagaki became warrant officers in the afterlife. Ensign Sakamaki, who had had the misfortune to fall alive into enemy hands, was studiously ignored in the praise and honours distributed after the operation. His bravery was, in the eyes of the Imperial Navy, cancelled out by his failure to sacrifice his life for the Emperor when placed in an impossible situation. To add insult to injury, the scuttling charge that Sakamaki had set inside his midget before abandoning ship had failed to detonate, and the Americans were able to recover an intact example of the Type-A to study.

As regards American preparedness concerning this new form of underwater warfare, the harbour defences were not impregnable to submarine attack even when carefully monitored. Although the Americans usefully would leave the gate in the harbour protective net wide open between 4.58 and 8.46 a.m., even if the gate had been firmly shut it would not have been impossible for the Japanese midget submarines to have penetrated Pearl Harbor. They could have passed beneath the net. According to Gordon W. Prange on 7 December 1941, the net extended to a depth of forty-five feet, but the harbour channel plunged down to a maximum depth of seventy-two feet. The Type-A midget was twenty feet tall, from the bottom of the keel to the top of the conning tower, and this would have given a midget seven feet of leeway beneath the net. Because the Americans left the net gate open for so long none of the five Japanese midgets was forced to attempt the tricky manoeuvre of passing under the net, but it remain theoretically possible, further demonstrating the usefulness of the Type-A in overcoming harbour defence measures.

The activities of the other submarines involved in the Pearl Harbor operation were similarly disappointing. The four boats of the 3rd Submarine Squadron achieved only two kills before returning to Kwajalein on 17 December. The *I-68* was damaged after being heavily depth-charged by American patrol boats thirty miles from the entrance to Pearl Harbor on 7 December, and the *I-69* ended up entangled in floating line off southern Oahu after an unsuccessful torpedo attack on a merchant ship. Whilst caught up the boat was also depth-charged, and the crew only managed to extricate their submarine by working flat out for forty hours. The boat came to the surface with the crew almost asphyxiated by the stale air onboard. The *I-72* managed to sink a small freighter 250 miles south of Oahu on 8 December, and the *I-75* made a similar claim when 100 miles south of Kauai on the 17th. The seven submarines forming the 1st Submarine Squadron under Rear-Admiral Sato only managed to sink one merchant ship on 11 December. The seven ocean cruising boats of 2nd Submarine Squadron would continue patrols until 11 January 1942. The *I-7* successfully conducted a dawn reconnaissance of battered Pearl Harbor on 17 December, the E14Y1 floatplane obtaining enough data to enable a complete damage report to be sent to Tokyo. Three days previously the *I-4* had sunk the 4,858-ton Norwegian merchant ship *Hoegh Merchant* off Makapuu Point, Oahu.

Later, the Japanese had endeavoured to find and destroy the American aircraft carriers that they had missed during the Pearl Harbor attack, and in January 1942 a Japanese submarine had torpedoed the USS *Saratoga* 500 miles west of Hawaii. The *Saratoga*, though damaged, survived to fight again, and on every occasion Japanese Naval Intelligence discovered the possible locations of American aircraft carriers all forces were directed towards locating and sinking them, often to the detriment of submarine operations then in play. This kind of strategy continued to demonstrate that in the Japanese Navy's mind submarines were vessels designed to work in close cooperation with the surface fleet, taking them away from the more valuable, with hindsight, tasks of sinking Allied merchant ships. The Japanese resolutely refused to use their submarine force in a similar fashion to the Germans, often with terrible results for the submarines employed against the increasingly technologically advanced anti-submarine detection equipped Allied warships.

The Japanese determined to understand why their massively potent submarine service deployed during and after the Pearl Harbor operation had failed to achieve the kind of impact expected. One reason was a command structure that saw the commander of 6th Fleet submarines, Admiral Shimizu, ensconced firmly on dry land at his headquarters in Kwajalein. Shimizu was simply too far removed from the situation to make much impact, or to have changed plans while the operation was ongoing. The overall commander also had a penchant for sending radio messages to his submarines when they were laying in position around Hawaii before the attack, alerting the Americans to a suspicious build-up of Japanese forces in the region. The Americans took care in routing merchant ships away from the reported locations of Japanese submarines, thereby limiting the boats' abilities to find and sink targets around the islands when war came. Planning was rather uncoordinated, with much of the potential the submarines posed being squandered, leading to all the glory going to the Imperial Naval Air Service. A final factor that upset the Japanese sub-surface plan was the unexpected strength of American anti-submarine forces, emphasized by the fate of the Special Attack Force midget submarines.

Notes

1. Peggy Warner & Sadao Seno, *The Coffin Boats: Japanese Midget Submarine Operations in the Second World War*, (London: Secker & Warburg Ltd), 1986, p.28
2. Paul Kemp, *Underwater Warriors: The Fighting History of Midget Submarines*, (London: Cassell Military Paperbacks), 2001
3. *I-16, I-18, I-20, I-22* and *I-24*
4. Gordon W. Prange with Donald M. Goldstein and Katherine V. Dillon, *Dec. 7 1941: The Day the Japanese Attacked Pearl Harbor*, (London: Harrap Limited), 1988, p.50
5. Warner and Seno, op. cit., p.37
6. Prange, Goldstein and Dillon, op. cit., p.50
7. *Report of the Joint Committee on the Investigation of the Pearl Harbor attack, Congress of the United States*, (Washington, DC: Government Printing Office), 1946, p. 58

Chapter 3

Target California

SOS, SOS: Under attack by enemy sub.
SS *Emidio*, California coast, 20 December 1941

Japanese 6th Fleet Headquarters at Kwajalein had come up with a further innovative use for submarines that had already been employed in the attack on Pearl Harbor. The seven submarines of 1st Submarine Squadron were given a new task, and were to bring the war in the Pacific to America's doorstep. Joined by the *I-10* and *I-26* from the original Pearl Harbor Reconnaissance Unit, Vice-Admiral Shimizu ordered the nine submarines to pursue the enemy eastwards and to patrol off the American west coast. The American public and military were already jittery following the audacious Japanese aerial and submarine attack on Hawaii, and rumours abounded of the likely next move by the Japanese towards the mainland of the United States. Perhaps an enemy landing on the lightly defended Pacific coasts of California or Oregon was a distinct possibility? The Japanese knew of American invasion fears and the redeployment of Japanese submarines close to these very coasts would hopefully have an adverse effect on civilian morale far outweighing any strategic or military impact they would have been able to make with the limited resources placed at their disposal.

Each of the eventual eight Japanese submarines that moved into position was ordered to interdict American coastal shipping by lying off the major shipping lanes, such as those located off Los Angeles and San Francisco.[1] Rear-Admiral Sato, commander of 1st Submarine Squadron, was aboard his flagship, the *I-9*, directing operations at sea. It was expected that each skipper would make each of his seventeen torpedoes tell, and 6th Fleet had ordered them to only expend one torpedo per enemy ship. The submarine captains had also been ordered to expend all of the ammunition for their submarine's 140mm deck-gun before returning to base. This would be achieved by supplementing the limited supply of torpedoes carried onboard by blasting merchant ships to pieces with the submarine's artillery piece, and then turning the gun on vulnerable American coastal installations. It was a plan intended to spread fear and panic along the huge Pacific Ocean coast of the United States, a plan to set the inshore waters and shoreline ablaze.

The *I-17* was a Type-B1 Japanese fleet submarine skippered by Lieutenant-Commander Kozo Nishino, an example of the most common and numerous class of submarine employed by Japan during the Second World War. Between 1940 and 1943 twenty were constructed, earlier examples such as the *I-17* being equipped with the ingenious Yokosuka E14Y1 floatplane used for reconnaissance. A watertight hanger was fitted aft of the conning tower, the aircraft being launched by means of a catapult and ramp built into the submarine's deck. Each B1 submarine was 356.5 feet long with a top speed on the surface of 23.5 knots, or 8 knots submerged and running on electric motors. Prior to the introduction of nuclear-powered submarines in the 1950s the vessels that fought in the Second World War were essentially submersibles rather than true submarines. Japanese, German, British and American submarines, and the submarines of every nation able to maintain undersea fleets, were all limited by their central power sources. Submarines at this stage were powered by diesel engines while they were at the surface, making them relatively fast and ideal platforms to launch anti-commerce and anti-warship attacks from, especially when cloaked by the cover of darkness. The power of large Japanese diesels fitted to many types of their submarines produced enough speed to allow the vessels to keep pace with the surface battle fleet – which remained a primary consideration of Japanese submarine designers throughout the Second World War. If forced below the surface of the water, or if attempting a submerged attack, the submarine was powered by electric motors running off cumbersome and space consuming batteries. The submarine immediately lost its speed and agility beneath the sea, and could only remain submerged while the air aboard remained breathable for the crew. The Japanese would not be able to match the Germans in advanced submarine design during the Second World War to overcome the twin problems of increasing underwater speed and staying semi-permanently submerged during patrols, and their submarine force would pay a heavy price as Allied anti-submarine technology developed exponentially as the war progressed. The Germans went some way to overcoming the problems of extended periods spent below the surface and running on electric motors by the incorporation of a Dutch design known as the snorkel. Basically, a submarine was fitted with a large mast that could be raised until the head was above the surface of the water, the submarine remaining submerged. Air would be sucked into the snorkel head, allowing the diesel engines to be run while the submarine was submerged, and the boat aired, theoretically enabling a German U-boat to conduct its patrol entirely submerged and therefore rendering it less vulnerable to Allied attacks. Fitted to most late-war German U-boats the snorkel often malfunctioned due to poor construction or components, and if waves splashed over the snorkel head the diesel engines would suck air from inside the U-boat, causing the crew great discomfort, especially to their ears and occasionally causing unconsciousness. Allied warships could also locate the snorkel head in the same way as a periscope mast, and the submarine would be attacked. Japanese submarines were not fitted with this technology, even though the Germans gave the Japanese detailed plans of the apparatus as part of ongoing German-Japanese trade and military technology exchanges between 1942 and 1945.

If a Type-B1 submarine was run at full speed on the surface the skipper would have rapidly used up his available diesel fuel, severely curtailing the boats operational potential, so a top speed was simply the boats potential power. Rather, a sensible skipper would be able to take his B1 on a round-trip patrol of approximately 14,000 nautical miles at a conservative 16 knots without requiring a single refuelling pit stop. This would make the B1 submarine the ideal platform with which to sail across the Northern Pacific to the west coast of the United States, and bring the war to America's doorstep. Added to the potency of the B1's great range was a 140mm deck-gun designed to assist a skipper in sinking ships. The deck-gun fired armour piercing anti-ship ammunition, designed to penetrate the steel hulls of ships and explode within. Pump a sufficient quantity of these cheap shells into a merchant ship and the result was a foregone conclusion, and just as effective as a torpedo. It was a more economical option than expending one of the seventeen torpedoes carried aboard the B1 through one of the boat's six torpedo tubes. Ninety-four officers and men crewed the B1, including two pilots and two observers to man the Yokosuka floatplane (one pilot and observer acting as a reserve crew).[2]

Although the B1 was not the biggest submarine type employed by the Imperial Navy, the Japanese nonetheless cornered the market in producing large submarines during the Second World War. The B1 was bigger, better armed, quicker and with a greater range than the closest comparable German U-boat type. For example, the Type IXC U-boat had given the Germans the ability to take the war to the east coasts of the United States, Canada and all around South Africa by 1942 and could motor an impressive 11,000 nautical miles at 12 knots before requiring refuelling. However, the Type IXC, at 252 feet long, was nearly 100 feet shorter than the Japanese B1, and was armed with fourteen torpedoes and a 105mm deck-gun and anti-aircraft weapons. Importantly, although German U-boats were smaller, had a shorter range and carried less munitions than their Japanese counterparts, they were quicker to submerge and were progressively equipped with superior technology such as radar detectors and snorkels that increased their survivability. The fundamental difference between a Japanese submarine and a German U-boat was not so much the technical specifications and technologies utilized in creating them, but the method in which they were employed. The Japanese viewed submarines as essentially fleet reconnaissance vessels to replace cruisers in that role, whereas the Germans saw submarines as the tool with which to sink millions of tons of enemy merchant shipping in order to reduce the industrial/military output of their opponents, and create hardship on the enemy home front.

Nishino aboard the *I-17* was proceeding on the surface in the pre-dawn darkness fifteen miles off Cape Mendocino, California on 18 December 1941, lookouts armed with powerful binoculars patiently scanning the barely discernable horizon on all points of the compass, and studying the sky in case of air attack. They were quiet, speaking only briefly in hushed tones, using their ears as well as their eyes to search out engine noises above the rhythmic reverberations of the *I-17*'s twin diesels as they lazily pushed them through the dark Pacific waters. The eerie red glow of low night lighting crept up the conning tower ladder from the control room below, etching the faces of the Japanese submariners into fixed masks of concentration and anticipation. Suddenly, as the first glow of dawn began to rise on the eastern horizon a lookout let out a guttural exclamation. His arm shot out in the direction of the approaching ship, a compass bearing relayed to the helmsman below, as Nishino ordered his vessel closed up and made ready for action. In normal circumstances a submarine captain would attack his intended target with a spread of torpedoes, a staggered shot that would fan out to intercept the intended target(s) after calculations of the speed and direction of the prey had been computed into the attack plot. Nishino was under strict orders to only expend a single torpedo per enemy ship, which did not give him much latitude for attack, and meant that the Japanese submarine would have to move up very close to the target ship to be sure of not wasting the valuable mechanical fish. Nishino decided that the best method of attack as the merchant ship hove into view was the employment of the deck-gun for the time being. If he could inflict sufficient damage to the freighter with his gun, enough to stop her, he could then decide whether to finish her off with more armour-piercing shells or close in for a single torpedo strike against a static target. The *I-17*, however, was rolling heavily in the swell as crewmen busily prepared the deck-gun for immediate action, manhandling shells from the gun's ready locker, ramming home a round with a solid thump as the breech was closed and the gun commander awaited the signal from the bridge to open fire.

The ship in the gunners' sights was the American freighter *Samoa* under the command of Captain Nels Sinnes, who was about to be abruptly awoken by the report of a submarine close by. The *Samoa* had already sustained damage, but not from enemy action. She had been caught by a heavy storm which had washed away one of the ship's lifeboats. The *Samoa* also had a noticeable list to port, as the engineers had been shifting water in the ballast tanks following the battering from the ocean. The pronounced list, and the remnants of the wooden lifeboat hanging from its launching davits, would be providential in saving the ship from the attentions of the *I-17* in the minutes that followed.

Captain Sinnes quickly dressed and, grasping a life jacket, ordered his crew to muster at their lifeboat stations. The sailors frantically stripped the covers from the open boats and began swinging them out on their davits ready to launch when the Japanese opened fire. Five times the *I-17*'s deck-gun barked, its flat high velocity report sounding out across the empty sea, the armour-piercing shells tearing towards the defenceless *Samoa*. Four missed to fountain in the choppy ocean, the Japanese gunners pitching hot, steaming shell cases overboard as others fetched fresh shells from the ready locker. The fifth shell exploded above the *Samoa* with an ear-splitting crack, white-hot shrapnel pummelling the deck. The Japanese submarine was rolling erratically on the disturbed sea, making it difficult for the gunners to accurately target the American ship, and they were reduced to flinging shells in the general direction of the enemy vessel and hoping for a lucky strike. Commander Nishino quickly tired of this pointless shooting and ordered a surfaced torpedo attack, the fish leaving the *I-17*'s bow with a hiss of compressed air and a trail of bubbles, quickly crossing the barely seventy yards that separated hunter and prey. In the early dawn light it appeared to the crews of both vessels to be a foregone conclusion.

Incredibly, as the crew of the *Samoa* braced for impact and a thunderous explosion, nothing happened. The torpedo passed clean underneath the merchant ship. The blind torpedo cruised on a short distance and then erupted in a massive tumult of water, smoke, fire and flying shrapnel. Fragments of the torpedo thumped harmlessly onto the *Samoa*'s deck, the *I-17* a low black shape that drifted ominously closer to the American ship. Officers aboard the submarine attempted to assess the damage the torpedo, which they erroneously assumed had struck the *Samoa*, had caused. Now perhaps no more than forty feet from the side of the merchant ship, the early morning gloom frustrated their efforts. Still the *I-17* closed with the *Samoa*, coming to within fifteen feet of the hull. Someone aboard the *I-17*, according to the Americans, yelled out in English 'Hi ya!' Captain Sinnes yelling back 'What do you want of us?' when he already knew the answer. From his position alongside the *Samoa* Nishino observed the vessel's heavy port list and assumed she was doomed. The *I-17* slowly pulled away and disappeared. Nishino instructed his radio operator to report a successful kill to the *I-15*, coordinating submarine operations from her position off San Francisco.[3]

The *Samoa* arrived safely in San Diego on 20 December after her close encounter, saved by storm damage and the poor early dawn light. On the same day Nishino redirected his submarine to its original position off Cape Mendocino, some twenty miles from the American coast. The crew of the *I-17* awaited another target of opportunity, buoyed up by their apparent first successful sinking of an enemy vessel of the mission. The day wore on with no sightings of American merchant ships, until, bathed by early afternoon winter sunshine, the lookouts were once more laboriously scanning the horizon and biding their time. Nishino made no attempt to disguise his presence so close to the coast, believing he had little to fear from American naval or air forces still reeling from the devastating attack on Pearl Harbor fourteen days previously. Just after 1.30 p.m. the sight of the oil tanker *Emidio* heading towards San Francisco rewarded Nishino's patience. The *Emidio* was only carrying ballast, returning empty from Seattle's Socony-Vacuum Oil Company facility.

Captain Clark Farrow reacted as swiftly as he could to the report of a submarine gaining on his ship. Nishino aboard the *I-17* ordered full power, the big diesels churning confidently ahead, the submarine making fully 20 knots, her exhausts trailing blue clouds of fumes into the clear Pacific air. Captain Farrow lightened his ship, dumping ballast that made the *Emidio* steady in the water but painfully slow, frantically ringing 'full speed ahead' on the engine room telegraph. The *I-17* cut through the water, closing rapidly on the *Emidio*'s stern, crew racing to man the deck-gun as Nishino manoeuvred his boat for the attack. It was imperative that the American ship be prevented from radioing for assistance, and therefore reporting Nishino's position to United States forces. Captain Farrow was already a step ahead of Nishino, however, as he had ordered his radio operator to send the following short Morse message: 'SOS, SOS: Under attack by enemy sub.'[4]

Nishino ordered the gun crew into action, the first shell exploding close to the *Emidio*'s radio antenna, blowing the fragile communication mast into useless scrap. In rapid succession the submarine's gun banged twice more, the shells screaming across the ocean into the defenceless *Emidio*, a lifeboat exploding into smouldering matchwood. Ashore, the US Army Air Corps were already scrambling a pair of medium bombers following the receipt of the *Emidio*'s distress signal and position, in the hope of destroying the Japanese submarine. Captain Farrow realized his ship was doomed, as the bombers would take some time to arrive, and he ordered the engines stopped. Meanwhile, the plucky radio operator had managed to restore communications with the shore by erecting a makeshift antenna. A white flag was hastily run up a mast and the tanker gradually slowed. The crew worked feverishly to swing out the remaining lifeboats while under constant shellfire from the *I-17*, Nishino ignoring the white flag and refusing to give the merchant seamen time to depart in the boats. It was not long before another shell found its mark, blowing three unfortunate crewmen into the water as it ploughed into their lifeboat. Twenty-nine crewmen were crowded aboard the lifeboats and pulled hard on the oars in an attempt to get clear of the *Emidio*, while four men, including the resourceful radio operator, remained aboard the ship, perhaps from a refusal to give up the vessel, or out of ignorance of the order to abandon ship issued by the captain.

On board the *I-17* lookouts had reported two black dots approaching from the mainland, which could only mean aircraft. Nishino ordered the bridge cleared, the submariners hastily clattering down into the pressure hull, securing the hatches as the submarine blew its tanks and slid beneath the waves in a swirl of white water. The *Emidio*'s remaining crewmen now turned their eyes skyward as the American bombers roared in low over the stricken merchantman. The two aircraft circled the spot where the *I-17* had a moment before submerged, eventually releasing a single depth charge. The *I-17* lurched violently as the depth charge detonated, but it was not close enough to cause the submarine any damage. Perhaps realizing that the American aircraft lacked the wherewithal and experience to launch a more devastating and coordinated anti-submarine attack Nishino did the opposite of most submarine skippers in his position. Ordering the *I-17* to periscope depth Nishino swiftly relocated the fully stopped *Emidio*. Orders were issued to partially surface the boat, and a torpedo was launched at the stationary American ship 200 yards distant. The torpedo ran true, impacting in the *Emidio*'s stern and detonating inside the ship with a massive blast of fire, smoke and debris. The *Emidio* lurched over as the engine room rapidly filled with freezing seawater. The torpedo claimed two of the four crewmen who had not vacated the ship earlier, and a third was injured. The radio operator, topside in his shack, frantically transmitted 'Torpedoed in the stern' before throwing himself clear of the ship into the sea. The surviving engineer, though wounded, also managed to struggle clear of the *Emidio*, and along with the radio operator he was plucked to safety by the small flotilla of lifeboats standing off the tanker.[5]

The *I-17* slipped once more beneath the waves as the two American bombers roared in to resume their ineffectual attack. Another depth charge plummeted into the sea and detonated in a giant plume of white water, concentric circles created by the sonic force of the explosion pushing out from the epicentre. The *I-17* escaped damage once more and motored quietly away from the scene, sure again of a confirmed kill.

The *Emidio*, though grievously wounded and abandoned by her crew, drifted off with the current. Lost for several days from human eyes, this Second World War *Mary Celeste* eventually ground up against jagged rocks opposite Crescent City, California, over eighty miles from her encounter with the *I-17*. As for her crew, their ordeal was to be sixteen hours in open boats and battling through an unsettling rainstorm before rescue by the US Coast Guard lightship *Shawnee* located off Humboldt Bay.

The *I-23*, another Type-B1 Japanese submarine with orders to sink unescorted American merchant ships, was active at the same time as the *I-17* was attempting to sink the tanker *Emidio*. Constructed at the Yokosuka Navy Yard, the *I-23* had entered service in September 1941. She was just in time to play a crucial part in 'Operation Z', the submarine contribution to the Japanese victory at Pearl Harbor. On 13 December the *I-23* began her relocation from the waters off Hawaii for the west coast of the United States.

On 20 December the *I-23* was approximately twenty miles off Monterey Bay, California, and with a target in sight. The American tanker *Agwiworld*, a 6,771-tonner belonging to the Richmond Oil Company was the Japanese target. Like a fighter pilot swooping down on a hapless rookie opponent, Lieutenant-Commander Shibata approached the oblivious *Agwiworld* with the early afternoon sun behind his boat, a classic attack from out of the sun. Coupled with a heavy swell the big Japanese submarine's approach behind the tanker was unobserved. The first the *Agwiworld* and her captain, Frederick Goncalves, knew of the presence of the Japanese submarine was the thump of the impact and explosion of a 140mm armour-piercing shell in the ship's stern. The *I-23* moved into a firing position to enable her deck-gunners to blast the tanker to scrap. However, due to the rough conditions, the Japanese sailors experienced difficulties loading and aiming the deck-gun. The *I-23*'s deck was awash as the boat rolled and pitched in the swell. Captain Goncalves did everything he could to make the *Agwiworld* as difficult a target as possible to hit, zigzagging through the whistling shells, probably eight or nine of them, before the *I-23* was seen to submerge.[6] Commander Shibata had clearly lost interest in his prey. The heavy seas and the fact that in order to achieve a good attacking position he would have had to have driven the *I-23* harder would have risked the lives of his gunners, who could have been swept overboard. A further factor which precluded a more determined assault on the tanker originated in the submarine's own radio room. The operator alerted his captain to the fact that the enemy ship had reported the Japanese submarine's attack to the US Navy, and assistance in the form of anti-submarine assets were undoubtedly on their way.

Shibata and the crew of the *I-23* were frustrated as they departed from the scene of their first attack on an American ship to search out further prey. Some time later Shibata encountered the 2,119-ton American merchant ship *Dorothy Phillips*. Employing an identical method of attack as that used against the *Agwiworld*, gunners again pumped high velocity armour piercing rounds into the hapless steamer. Although the *I-23* successfully disabled the *Dorothy Phillips*'s steering by wrecking the ship's rudder with a shell strike, a torpedo attack was not pressed home, presumably because the sea conditions were still unfavourable. Nevertheless, the *Dorothy Phillips* eventually ran aground so Shibata had scored a victory of sorts.[7]

Lieutenant-Commander Kanji Matsumura was an experienced submarine skipper, having previously commanded the *RO-65, RO-66* and *RO-61* before commissioning the *I-21* into service on 15 July 1941. As with the other boats assigned to operations along the United States west coast, the *I-21* was formerly part of the submarine task group that made up an element of 'Operation Z'. On 9 December the submarine *I-6* had reported a Lexington-class aircraft carrier and two cruisers heading north-east. The Japanese were well aware that although they had scored a notable victory against the US Pacific Fleet's battleship squadron they had failed to sink or damage a single American aircraft carrier. It was imperative that American carriers be sunk or damaged wherever found for the Japanese themselves had already demonstrated the power of naval aviation in this new conflict, and the days of the big-gun battleship appeared to be numbered. Vice-Admiral Shimizu at 6th Fleet Headquarters at Kwajalein, on receiving the intelligence report from the *I-6*, immediately ordered all submarines not involved with the launching of the midget submarines during the Pearl Harbor operation, known as the Special Attack Force, to proceed at flank speed and sink the American carrier. The *I-21* was included in Shimizu's force sent to intercept the vessel later identified as the USS *Enterprise*, but her progress was hampered by problems with the submarine's diesel engines and electrics. Carrier-based Douglas SBD Dauntless aircraft spotted the *I-21* on the surface on a number of occasions, necessitating Matsumura to crash-dive. Matsumura became increasingly fed up with constantly being forced beneath the waves by patrolling American aircraft. He decided upon a bold course of action – to remain surfaced and take on the enemy aircraft with his anti-aircraft armament. Motoring on the surface at 1 p.m. on the afternoon of 13 December a lone Dauntless attacked the submarine from the port side, but the accuracy of the Japanese anti-aircraft barrage caused the pilot to abort his attack run and go around for a second attempt. Diving towards the port side of the submarine again the American aircraft released a single bomb which slammed into the sea close to the *I-21*, but which failed to detonate.

Following the unsuccessful operation to intercept and sink the *Enterprise* and her escorts, on 14 December Matsumura and the *I-21* were assigned a new patrol area off Point Arguello in California, a promontory of land fifty-five miles north of Santa Barbara. Motoring just below the surface close to the shore on the morning of 22 December, Commander Matsumura spotted the *H. M. Story*, a Standard Oil Company tanker, as he scanned the horizon at periscope depth. For two days the *I-21* had waited in this position, only coming to the surface at night to recharge the submarine's batteries and air the boat. Lookouts aboard the *H. M. Story* never spied the periscope mast cutting through the waves, as the instrument's blank gaze determined the American ship's speed and course. Matsumura now seized his opportunity and ordered the *I-21* to surface. The bulky submarine rose majestically to the surface, ballast tanks blowing noisily and hatches clanking metallically as officers and men manned the conning tower bridge and the deck-gun, the air thick with bellowed commands. As Matsumura and his officers fixed the *H. M. Story* in their binoculars the submarine's deck-gun blazed into life.

Witnesses ashore said they saw a torpedo running in the sea, as the *I-21* was between the *H. M. Story* and the quiet beach at Point Arguello. The tanker was approximately three miles from the shoreline. What had first attracted the witnesses' attention was the report of the submarine's deck-gun, but the gunners view of the target was quickly obscured by thick black smoke emitted from the *H. M. Story* as the vessel attempted to avoid destruction. What was believed to have been a torpedo was observed rapidly exiting the smoke screen as the *H. M. Story* went full ahead. The Japanese Long Lance torpedo shot through the water towards the tanker, occasionally coming to the surface, slapping white spray off the tops of the waves as it did so. Matsumura was once more unsuccessful as the torpedo passed in front of the tanker.[8] This indicates again the limiting effect of the order issued to submarine commanders to only expend one torpedo per merchant ship. If the German method of firing a spread of two or three torpedoes had been employed the *H. M. Story*, and probably many other merchant ships throughout the region, would have almost certainly been struck. The use of the deck-gun to attempt to wreck a merchant ship's communications equipment, as well as hasten the ship's sinking, was also proving to be a suspect attack method. The *H. M. Story* was able to radio for assistance, and shore-based US Army Air Corps bombers quickly arrived on the scene. These aircraft dropped several bombs in an attempt to destroy the now submerged *I-21*, but without effect. More importantly, however, was the fact that Matsumura had intercepted and failed to sink two American tankers, on each occasion being forced to give up the hunt and slink off frustrated to attempt to locate some other target.

North of Point Arguello along the coast is the little town of Cayucas, and by the early morning of 23 December the *I-21* was sitting quietly on the surface off the settlement, all eyes scanning the horizon. At 3 a.m. lookouts spotted the *Larry Doheny*, a twenty-year old empty Richmond Oil Company tanker skippered by Captain Roy Brieland. The *Larry Doheny* was six miles off Cayucas when Matsumura attempted once again to disable a ship with his deck-gun. The first shot roused the crew aboard the *Larry Doheny*, Captain Brieland frantically ordering the helmsman to deviate from his course and begin zigzagging in a desperate attempt to throw the Japanese gunners off target. In fact, Brieland's evasive manoeuvres had almost succeeded in stalling Matsumura's attack, for the Japanese skipper, after two shots had missed from his deck-gun, was about to issue the order to curtail the attack. The *I-21* was hampered by both darkness and by Brieland's violent evasive manoeuvring of his ship. However, at the last moment a lookout reported the enemy ship to be less than 200 yards from the submarine, and, importantly, exposing her port side. Matsumura ordered an immediate torpedo attack, the Long Lance quickly crossing the water between the two vessels. However, luck was on Brieland's side, for as the *Larry Doheny* made another turn the Japanese torpedo sailed past the tanker and exploded some way off, the massive detonation clearly audible to the citizens of Cayucas already woken by the firing of the submarine's deck-gun.[9] With the expending of a torpedo Matsumura followed his standing orders and broke off the attack. The *Larry Doheny* had survived, but was, ironically, to come to grief at the hands of another Japanese submarine the following year, also off the west coast.

At 3 a.m. that same morning the 8,272-ton Union Oil Company tanker *Montebello* pulled away from the dockside at Port San Luis, California. She was bound for the Canadian port of Vancouver in British Columbia with a mixed cargo of oil and petrol. The bulk of her cargo, however, consisted of 4.1 million gallons of heavy crude oil loaded into ten separate storage tanks.[10] Her captain, Olaf Eckstrom, placed her on course, not realizing that his route would bring his ship into the sights of the *I-21* less than two hours later. He, and other merchant skippers, had received no warnings from the US Navy or the Coast Guard regarding prowling Japanese submarines that had already made several attacks on coastal shipping.

Commander Matsumura must have felt a dull rage at his failure to sink two defenceless American ships, both of which should have been easy kills for the big *I-21*. As the *I-21* motored further north the search resumed once more for targets of opportunity, and that elusive first successful kill of the mission. At 5.30 a.m. Captain Eckstrom aboard the *Montebello* was informed that what appeared to be a submarine was stalking his vessel. Eckstrom went immediately to investigate and there was no mistaking the size and outline of a big submarine closing on the ship's stern. Eckstrom followed the only anti-submarine direction at his disposal and ordered the helmsman to begin zigzagging in the hope of throwing the submarine's aim off target, the same manoeuvre that had saved the *Larry Doheny* from destruction. After ten minutes Eckstrom realized that the manoeuvre was a futile gesture. The *I-21* was closer than ever, and a Long Lance exited the submarine when the *Montebello* was broadside to her. With a blinding flash and a tremendous explosion the torpedo impacted amidships, the *Montebello* shuddering perceptively as the tanker slowed. It seemed clear to the crew aboard that the *Montebello* had been struck a fatal blow from which the only recourse was to abandon ship in the four wooden lifeboats available. Incredibly, through sheer good luck, the Japanese torpedo had struck the only compartment that was empty of oil or petrol. Had it struck elsewhere it is doubtful if more than a handful of the thirty-six men aboard would have survived the resultant inferno. What many crewmen remembered most was the courage under fire displayed by their Scandinavian skipper. And Eckstrom had only been promoted to captain one hour before the *Montebello* had departed port, when he was serving as first mate and the original captain had suddenly resigned. Eckstrom was 'as cool as a snowdrift' recalled the new first mate as he stood on the deck and ordered his crew to their lifeboats, and then gave the order to abandon ship.[11] For his part, Eckstrom was not entirely convinced the *Montebello* was done for, and ordered the lifeboats to be rowed a distance from the vessel, and told the crew to sit on their oars and wait. Hopefully the Japanese submarine would depart, and perhaps the *Montebello* could be re-boarded if she was not discovered to be foundering. Commander Matsumura, however, had darker ideas concerning the fate of the American crew.

Even as the crew was taking to the lifeboats the Japanese opened fire on the *Montebello* with their deck-gun, firing approximately ten rounds at the listing vessel as the crew began to lower themselves over the side in their boats. Clearly, to Matsumura's mind, the crew was expendable as the object of the attack was to make sure the *Montebello* went to the bottom. This kind of cold-blooded assault was characteristic of Japanese naval operations throughout the Second World War, and was repeated on countless occasions. It is in direct contrast to the behaviour of German U-boat crews, who very often gave merchant seamen time to abandon their ship before finishing off a vessel with a torpedo or the deck-gun. Eckstrom and his crew rowed a distance from the *Montebello*, by another stroke of good fortune suffering no injuries from flying shrapnel as round after round hammered into the stricken tanker, and within forty-five minutes the *Montebello* had slid beneath the waves. Eckstrom now ordered his crew to begin pulling for the shore. They were some four miles from the Piedras Blancas lighthouse.[12]

Matsumura had achieved the first kill of his mission to the United States west coast, but what followed was an attempt to murder the American sailors in their lifeboats. Machine guns were brought up into the conning tower of the submarine and fire was poured forth on the helpless lifeboats pulling hard for the coast. It was only poor visibility that saved the crew of the

Montebello from murder at the hands of the Japanese, and Matsumura eventually ordered the submarine to leave the vicinity of the attack. Machine-gun bullets had struck lifeboats, though fortunately the crewmen sheltering inside them had not been injured. Although the malevolent Japanese submarine had departed, the hapless crew of the *Montebello* faced a new battle for survival in attempting to row lifeboats holed by machine-gun rounds to the shore through a heavy sea. Men took turns pulling on the oars or bailing water from their boats until, utterly exhausted, around noon they washed up on the beach opposite the town of Cambria.

Why the Japanese were intent on murdering the civilian crewmen of a vessel they had successfully sunk has an explanation. It was official policy even though it violated laws to which the Japanese were themselves signatories. According to Lord Russell of Liverpool's seminal work *The Knights of Bushido: A Short History of Japanese War Crimes* [13] when Japan had signed the 1922 London Naval Treaty, Article 22 of that agreement provided that submarine actions must conform to International Law, and that 'except in the case of persistent refusal to stop on being duly summoned, or of active resistance to visit and search, warships, whether surface vessel or submarine may not sink or render incapable of navigation a merchant vessel without having first placed passengers, crew and ship's papers in a place of safety'. A 'place of safety' in the case of the *Montebello* was the ship's lifeboats. The Japanese had allowed the 1922 Treaty to expire on 31 December 1936, but Article 22 remained binding on all signatories, 'by virtue of Article 23, which laid down in Part IV of the expiring Treaty relating to submarines should remain in force without time limit'. So even though Japan considered the treaty expired, the section concerning submarine action remained in force forever, because it accorded with basic International Law. Further to this, Lord Russell also points out that Japan had signed a further Protocol in London on 6 November 1936 with the United States, Great Britain (including the Dominions and Empire), France and Italy, which incorporated verbatim the very provisions of Part IV of the 1922 Treaty relating to the conduct of submarines in war. Interestingly, Commander Matsumura's actions regarding the crew of the *Montebello* actually predated the accepted change in Japanese government and naval policy towards merchant ship crews. His actions, however, certainly conform to the de facto attitude of the Imperial Navy to non-combatants. It was only following talks between Lieutenant-General Hiroshi Oshima, Japanese Ambassador to Germany, and Adolf Hitler in Berlin on 3 January 1942, a little under a month after the entry of the United States into the war, that Hitler suggested murdering surviving merchant ship crewmen. Although the German Navy flatly refused to entertain such a notion, Oshima was apparently sufficiently impressed by Hitler's argument that depriving the Americans of trained crewmen would undermine their massive shipbuilding capacity that he reported to the Japanese government that such a measure should be adopted. It duly was, in flagrant violation of the laws outlined above, on 20 March 1943, when submarine skippers were ordered to exterminate all survivors from sunken ships, and Imperial forces faithfully carried out this order. Matsumura's actions certainly predate the official order, but it is clear that either he was unaware of International Law and the agreements his country had signed regarding the correct behaviour of submarine skippers (which seems unlikely owing to his rank and experience), or that Matsumura and his contemporaries had been given tacit approval for such measures to be taken against helpless survivors. Subordinate Japanese military officers were not generally known for thinking for themselves, and following orders to the letter regardless of cost was very much the rule (one torpedo per merchant ship for example). It appears unlikely that Matsumura decided to murder some three dozen unarmed and defenceless sailors on a whim, or out of revenge for his earlier humiliation at failing to sink the *H. M. Story* and the *Larry Doheny*. There was a certain cold, calculated method in Matsumura's actions that could only have been sanctioned by a higher authority than he.

The consequences of Matsumura's sinking of the *Montebello* are still felt today. In 1996 the wreck of the tanker was located in 900 feet of water, sitting upright on the seabed adjacent to the Monterey Bay National Marine Sanctuary. A preliminary investigation of the wreck by a remotely operated vehicle (ROV) revealed that the Japanese torpedo had ruptured only two out of the *Montebello*'s ten oil storage tanks. The remaining eight tanks were still watertight, and full of millions of gallons of crude oil. As the wreck naturally deteriorates over time eventually that oil will be released into the surrounding ocean, which poses an alarming ecological issue for the nearby marine sanctuary. Salvaging the wreck has not been seriously considered due to the costs involved, so scientists can only regularly inspect the wreck for signs of degradation. Inevitably, this ghost of the Second World War sits rusting away, a potential ecological time bomb waiting to go off.

Commander Matsumura decided to remain in the vicinity of his successful sinking of the *Montebello*. He was rewarded later that day, 23 December, by the appearance of the 6,418-ton American tanker *Idaho*, which he shelled and damaged with his deck-gun before breaking off his attack. However, the following day Matsumura and the *I-21* came close to running foul of American anti-submarine forces in the region. The *I-21* was patrolling at periscope depth when a small, depth charge armed patrol vessel surprised her. Two depth charges were released which exploded close to the submarine's hull. The *I-21*'s vertical rudder was wrecked, and the explosions also knocked out all of her lights. Matsumura decided that instead of staying down and being bombarded to pieces by depth charges, the *I-21* would surface, enabling the gunners to fight it out with the patrol boat and any reinforcements that showed up. Matsumura's banzai tactic was forestalled just as the boat was rising to the surface as the lights suddenly came back on and the engineering department reported that they had repaired the submarine's steering. This meant that the *I-21* could be saved, and more importantly returned to Kwajalein for repairs. Matsumura immediately left the area and set a course for home. On 11 January 1942 the *I-21* arrived back at base, and Commander Matsumura was incorrectly credited with sinking two enemy tankers.[14]

On 14 December 1941, in common with the other Japanese submarines discussed throughout this chapter, the *I-25* was reassigned to the United States west coast. The *I-25* was given a patrol area off the cities of Astoria and Portland in Oregon, specifically targeting merchant shipping using the important Columbia River estuary. The *I-25* struck early on in the Japanese attempt to plague American coastal commerce, locating the Union Oil tanker *L. P. St. Clair*. Following standard operational orders issued to all submarine skippers before the commencement of the west coast campaign, the captain of the *I-25*, Lieutenant-Commander Meiji Tagami, assigned the job of sinking the tanker to his deck-gun crew. No torpedoes were used during the night time attack. As the gunners attempted to hit the *L. P. St. Clair* with gunfire, the captain put her hard to port and managed to evade ten armour-piercing rounds before disappearing into the dark Columbia River Channel.[15]

On 22 December Commander Tagami was offered something enticing in a radio message from 6th Fleet Headquarters at Kwajalein in the Marshall Islands. The Combined Fleet Intelligence Bureau had received information that the battleships USS *Mississippi, New Mexico* and *Idaho* were in the process of transferring into the Pacific from the Atlantic via the Panama Canal to reinforce the shattered US Pacific Fleet. Although this information would prove to be false, Vice-Admiral Shimizu immediately radioed the submarines *I-25, I-17* and *I-9*. Japanese naval intelligence estimated that the battleships were due to arrive at Los Angeles on or about Christmas Day 1941. The *I-25* was ordered to patrol the area between Los Angeles and San Francisco in the hope of intercepting the capital ships as they made their way to port. After the intelligence concerning the three American battleships had turned out to be false the *I-25* was ordered to patrol off the Oregon coast, to continue her original mission of commerce interdiction.

On 27 December the submarine's lookouts located the 8,684-ton American tanker *Connecticut* during the night off the aptly named Cape Disappointment. The lookouts saw the tanker's white masthead running light in the distance, and discerned her engine noise on the clear night air. Tagami gave immediate chase, spending twenty minutes manoeuvring into a suitable attack position before launching a single torpedo at the *Connecticut*'s stern. The Long Lance struck the tanker squarely in the stern, submarine and prey both brilliantly illuminated for a second by the flash of the explosion that immediately ignited a large fire. Tagami assumed that he had dealt the *Connecticut* a killer blow from which the tanker would not recover. Satisfied that the tanker would eventually sink, Tagami ordered the *I-25* to motor away from the scene some ten miles off the American coast. The *Connecticut*, however, although settling by the stern, was not ready to disappear just yet. She escaped the scene of the attack and eventually went aground in the mouth of the Columbia River where she was salvaged for repairs.[16] Once again, the single torpedo mantra being adhered to by Japanese submarine skippers was costing them their kills, though most commanders left the scene of their attacks believing that they had successfully sunk the ships they had struck.

Following the attack on the *Connecticut*, Tagami took the *I-25* back to base to refuel, rearm and revictual. On 11 January 1942 the *I-25* arrived at the 6th Fleet's anchorage at Kwajalein. On 8 February the submarine set sail again, this time bound not for America, but for the coasts of Australia and New Zealand.[17]

The *I-19* first struck at commercial traffic off the west coast early on Christmas Eve 1941. Completed at Kobe by Mitsubishi Shipbuilding in April 1941, the *I-19* under Lieutenant-Commander Shogo Narahara had already untaken duties during the Japanese attack on Pearl Harbor and the subsequent failed pursuit of the aircraft carrier USS *Enterprise*. For the move to the coast of the United States the *I-19* had been assigned a patrol area off the great metropolis of Los Angeles. On 22 December the *I-19* had chased the American oil tanker *H.M. Storey* for an hour before Narahara had been satisfied that his firing position was good. Disregarding orders concerning the use of torpedoes, Narahara ordered a spread of three released from the bow tubes, all of which missed the tanker. The *H.M. Storey* made good her escape and a frustrated Narahara continued his patrol, itching for another opportunity to prove his usefulness.

On the morning of Christmas Eve Commander Narahara sighted the *Barbara Olsen*, a freighter loaded down with lumber that was on her way to San Diego. The Long Lance torpedo released by the *I-19* passed clean beneath the *Barbara Olsen*, and detonated approximately 100 feet from the ship's hull. The booming detonation of the torpedo, and the massive column of black smoke which rose to 300 feet, was spied by lookouts aboard the US Navy sub chaser USS *Amethyst* that was patrolling the entrance to Los Angeles harbour four miles away from the aborted Japanese attack. The *Amethyst* immediately went to 'Action Stations' and raced to the assistance of the *Barbara Olsen*. On this occasion, although the *Amethyst* conducted a thorough search of the area, no trace was found of the offending submarine. In fact, Narahara had taken his boat several miles north to an area close to the lighthouse at Point Fermin. By 10 a.m. that Christmas Eve the *I-19* was settled down at periscope depth awaiting a target of opportunity to emerge from the nearby Catalina Channel. By 10.30 a.m. a 5,700-ton lumber freighter named *Absaroka* was observed by the *I-19* off Point Fermin.[18]

Commanded by Captain Louie Pringle, the McCormick Steamship Company vessel would pass within one mile of a US Army coastal defence gun position located in front of the Point Fermin lighthouse, the soldiers having a grandstand view of the events that followed. The *I-19* pressed home its attack on the *Absaroka* with determination. The first torpedo passed wide of the freighter, but a second torpedo was launched almost immediately, Commander Narahara continuing to disregard the 'one torpedo per enemy ship' order previously issued to the Japanese submarines operating off America. This second torpedo slammed into the *Absaroka*'s Number 5 Hold, the blast throwing three crewmen, busily engaged in checking that the lumber carried on deck was securely fastened down, overboard. Massive quantities of lumber were blown into the air by the force of the explosion, one crewman recalling that it appeared 'as if a man were throwing matchsticks around'.[19] One of the three crewmen flung into the water by the torpedo strike was able to get back aboard the *Absaroka* almost immediately. The ship heeled over in the blast, her main deck railing touching the surface of the sea. The seaman took a firm hold of the railing, and as the ship righted herself he was lifted clear of the water and scrambled back aboard. Another of the men who had gone overboard managed to climb back onto the deck with the aid of a rope. The third man had been injured during the explosion and would require assistance from his shipmates to get safely back aboard the ship. Standing on deck, Seaman Ryan picked up a rope mooring line and flung it at the man struggling in the water. However, in the midst of this rescue attempt a tragedy struck. The force of the torpedo's explosion had upset the tons of lumber stored on the freighter's deck, and the lashings holding everything securely in place had parted or were no longer tight. As Ryan concentrated on trying to save his comrade a massive pile of lumber suddenly broke free with a roar and fell upon him. Ryan was crushed to death and his body swept over the ship's side as tons of lumber splashed into the sea.

In the *Absaroka*'s radio shack the operator had picked himself up off the floor where he had been flung by the force of the Japanese torpedo impact and had sent an SOS distress call and details of the submarine attack to the shore. On deck, the remaining crew had already begun to make the ship's lifeboats ready as the *Absaroka* settled lower and lower in the water. Responding to the *Absaroka*'s distress call, US Army Air Corps planes soon arrived at the scene, dropping bombs into the sea close to the *I-19*'s last reported position. The USS *Amethyst* steamed defiantly up to the *Absaroka*, taking off the crew, and then spent several hours' depth charging the area in the vain hope of destroying the elusive Japanese submarine. It was all to no avail, as none of the thirty-two depth charges found their target. As time passed it became apparent to Captain Pringle that his ship, although with her main deck awash, was not in any immediate danger of foundering. Perhaps the *Absaroka* could be salvaged, and with this in mind a US Navy tug tied up to the freighter ready to haul her to land. Pringle and seven volunteers re-boarded the *Absaroka* to assist with the salvage operation. With great care the freighter was taken into shore and beached below Fort MacArthur. The great hole in the *Absaroka*'s hull made by the Japanese torpedo became a useful propaganda tool for the American home front. In a similar tone to the British slogan 'Careless talk costs lives', movie actress Jane Russell was photographed standing in the gaping hole holding a poster emblazoned with the slogan 'A slip of the lip may sink a ship.' The photograph appeared in *LIFE magazine* in January 1942.[20] The press speculated on the possible involvement of Japanese-Americans in assisting enemy submarines in finding their targets, all of which was completely unfounded and further demonstrated the fear and paranoia gripping the west coast.

By Christmas Day 1941 the Japanese submarines assigned to interdict American coastal shipping had begun to break off their attacks and plot a course for their home bases. Originally, all of the submarines were to have moved even closer inshore, and were supposed to have expended their deck-gun ammunition against shore installations along the west coast before heading home. Admiral Osami Nagano, Chief of the Naval General Staff in Tokyo, had countermanded Vice-Admiral Shimizu's original shore bombardment order. It has been surmised that Nagano feared that American submarines would retaliate by bombarding Japanese coastal installations and towns. Only Commander Nishino and the *I-17* would go against his wishes and conduct a coastal bombardment sortie against the United States before departing across the Pacific.

Notes

1. *I-26* – Cape Flattery, Washington; *I-25* – mouth of Columbia River, Oregon; *I-9* – Cape Blanco, Oregon; *I-17* – Cape Mendocino, California; *I-15* – San Francisco, California; *I-23* – Point Arguello, California; *I-19* – Los Angeles, California; *I-10* – San Diego, California
2. Data derived from Bob Hackett & Sander Kingsepp's http://www.combined-fleet.com
3. Bert Webber, *Silent Siege III: Japanese Attacks on North America in World War II: Ships Sunk, Air Raids, Bombs Dropped, Civilians Killed*, (Medford, OR: Webb Research Group), 1992
4. *The Attack on the SS Emidio*, The California State Military Museum, California State Military Department, http://www.militarymuseum.org
5. ibid.
6. Data derived from Bob Hackett & Sander Kingsepp's http://www.combined-fleet.com/I-23.htm
7. *The Attack on the SS Dorothy Phillips*, The California State Military Museum, California State Military Department, http://www.militarymuseum.org
8. Donald J. Young, '*West Coast War Zone*', *World War II*, http://historynet.com
9. ibid.
10. *The Attack on the SS Montebello*, The California State Military Museum, California State Military Department, http://www.militarymuseum.org
11. Young, op. cit.
12. ibid.
13. Lord Russell of Liverpool, *The Knights of Bushido: A Short History of Japanese War Crimes*, (London: Greenhill Books, Lionel Leventhal Limited), 2005, p.213.
14. Data derived from Bob Hackett & Sander Kingsepp's http://www.com-binedfleet.com/I-21.htm
15. Young, op. cit.
16. ibid.

17. Data derived from Bob Hackett & Sander Kingsepp's http://www.combinedfleet.com/I-25.htm
18. Data derived from Bob Hackett & Sander Kingsepp's http://www.combinedfleet.com/I-19.htm
19. Young, op. cit.
20. ibid.

Chapter 4

The Empire Strikes Back

The submarine made violent maneuvers [sic] *to lose contact, with the* EDSALL *trailing and attempting to make a good approach.*
Commander J.J. Nix, USS *Edsall*, 31 January 1942

HMAS *Deloraine* was a minesweeper of the Bathurst-class. Although officially designated a minesweeper the vessels of the class were actually known as corvettes. The *Deloraine* was one of sixty such vessels constructed by Australian shipyards during the Second World War. Twenty were ordered built by the Admiralty in London, but their crews were to be from the Royal Australian Navy and the vessels were commissioned in Australia. A further thirty-six Bathurst-class corvettes were specially built for the Royal Australian Navy, with another four constructed in Australia but serving with the Royal Indian Navy.

HMAS *Deloraine* was commissioned into service at a ceremony conducted in Sydney on 22 December 1941, after having been officially named and launched on 26 July by Dame Mary Hughes, wife of the Australian Navy Minister. The vessel was placed under Lieutenant-Commander Desmond Menlove of the Royal Australian Naval Reserve. The eighty-four officers and men under Menlove lived aboard a vessel 186 feet in length, and which weighed only 650 tons. The *Deloraine* was powered by two triple-expansion diesel engines that generated 2,000 horsepower, and which gave the anti-submarine corvette a maximum speed of 15 knots. At the time of the *Deloraine*'s entanglement with the Japanese submarine *I-124* her main armament consisted of a single 12-pounder gun (later beefed up with the addition of a 4-inch gun). She also boasted three Oerlikon cannon and machine guns, although later in her career this armament configuration was modified by the removal of an Oerlikon gun and its replacement with a more powerful 37mm Bofors gun. The *Deloraine*'s anti-submarine capability was expressed by the depth charge chutes and throwers located in her stern.

On 26 December 1941 HMAS *Deloraine* sailed out of Sydney and headed north, bound for Darwin in the Northern Territory. She would begin her career by undertaking a period of anti-submarine patrol duty in the Arafura Sea. She arrived in Darwin on 7 January 1942 and immediately began work patrolling the entrance to Darwin Harbour. The Australians rightly suspected that Japanese submarines were operating in the area around Darwin, and by January 1942 the Japanese were pushing their southern flank virtually into Australian coastal waters. The submarine *I-124* was lurking close to Darwin, dropping mines and hoping for a chance to torpedo an enemy ship entering or exiting Darwin, Australia's most important northern port. The boat was an I-121-Class minelaying submarine. Only four vessels of this class were completed, and the Kure Naval Shipyard had constructed the *I-124* in 1928. Each of the four vessels measured 279 feet in length and displaced 1,383 tons. They were powered by diesel engines that generated 2,400 horsepower, and for submerged travel the boat was powered by electric motors of 1,200 horsepower. They were roughly equivalent in size and power to the German Type IX U-boat, though slightly slower and with a bigger crew. The *I-124* had a maximum surface speed of 14 knots, or a respectable 9.5 knots when submerged. A complement of eighty officers and men crewed the boat, under Lieutenant-Commander Kouichi Kishigami.

The *I-124*'s armament consisted of four torpedo tubes, a 150mm deck-gun, and forty-two mines. Although the submarine was more than capable of interdicting Allied shipping using torpedoes or deck-gun bombardment, her primary task, and the role for which the vessels of her class had been designed and constructed, was to lay mines along enemy shipping channels. Throughout January 1942 the sister ships of the *I-124* (the *I-121, I-122* and *I-123*) were all active in mining Australian inshore waters. The *I-121* had laid thirty-nine mines around the Joseph Bonaparte Gulf area 125 miles south-west of Darwin on 12

January. The *I-122* dropped thirty mines in the western approaches to the Torres Strait around 15 January, and her sister submarine, the *I-123*, deposited a further thirty mines in the Dundas Strait off Cape Don on the Coburg Peninsula. The *I-124* herself had deposited twenty-seven mines close to Darwin before her terminal encounter with HMAS *Deloraine*. The mines that the Japanese submarines sowed were German, a type known as the TMC. The TMC had first appeared in 1940, originally designed for use on land with influence fusing, but later adapted for use at sea. The naval version could be placed in waters up to 37 metres in depth, and each mine had an explosive charge of between 1,896 and 2,050 pounds of TNT. Some of the mines laid by Japanese submarines were still being washed up in Australia during the mid-1960s.

On 20 January 1942 Commander Kishigami discovered the American fleet oiler USS *Trinity* close to the port of Darwin. The *Trinity* was accompanied by the destroyer escort USS *Edsall*. Kishigami was a bold commander, but he was perhaps also aware of the eyes of his own commanding officer judging his actions. Along for the patrol of the *I-124* as an observer was Kishigami's division commander, Captain Keiyu Endo. Port Darwin at this time contained over forty Allied ships, and the presence of Captain Endo suggests that the operation was high-priority, and perhaps intended to interdict trade in and out of Darwin. It is also suggested from the later reports of one of the ships involved in the sinking of the *I-124* that another Japanese submarine may have also been present, perhaps forming a small flotilla under Endo's overall command.

Three torpedoes were fired at the *Trinity* in a spread, but quick evasive action by the oiler witnessed all three miss their target. The attack also alerted the *Edsall*, which immediately, in the words of her skipper, 'sheared violently to port reversing course and maneuvered to screen between submarine and *TRINITY*'.[1] At 6.37 a.m. the *Edsall* located a submarine at a distance of 2,300 yards, but the destroyer USS *Alden* chased the submarine down a sonar contact bearing, plastering the area with a barrage of depth charges while the *Edsall* continued to screen the *Trinity*. Contact with the submarine was then lost, owing to the nature of depth charging. When a depth charge exploded it disrupted the ship's sonar equipment for up to fifteen minutes, meaning the operator was forced to wait until he could achieve a fresh fix on the target. In some cases, submarines that survived the initial depth charge attack were able to use the attacker's resultant sonar 'blindness' to hastily exit the scene. The *Edsall* was ordered by the *Trinity* to take up station ahead of the convoy while the *Trinity* made a contact report to the local Australian Commander Base Force in Port Darwin informing him of her attack on a submarine, but the *Trinity*'s captain did not know whether the *Alden* had inflicted any damage.

HMAS *Deloraine* was at sea when reports came in of a contact between a US Navy destroyer and an enemy submarine. Command immediately contacted Menlove and ordered him to take his vessel on a prearranged patrol line, factoring in the position of the earlier attack that would hopefully bring the *Deloraine* into contact with the enemy. By 1.35 p.m. the *Deloraine* was patrolling the assigned area after having raced to the scene at a near maximum speed of 14.5 knots. It was Kishigami, however, aboard the *I-124*, who made the opening move. Lining up on the little corvette a single torpedo was fired, lookouts aboard the *Deloraine* spotting the torpedo's distinctive white wake as it ploughed through the waves towards them. A shout of 'torpedo in the water!' followed by the bearing, estimated range and speed gave Menlove just enough time to order the helmsman to take evasive action. The torpedo rocketed past the stern, missing by just ten feet, as the *Deloraine* came about. If the torpedo had impacted the *Deloraine*'s stern, loaded down as it was with depth charges, half the ship would have been blown off and dozens of the crew killed or injured.

In the meantime the sonar operator aboard the *Deloraine* informed the bridge that he had a good echo contact on the submarine, allowing Menlove to manoeuvre his ship ready to launch a volley of depth charges. On board the *I-124*, Kishigami must have realized the terrible danger his vessel and crew were now in as his opening gambit with the torpedo attack had failed. Every man aboard the submarine could hear the *Deloraine*'s engines growing louder, and every man knew what inevitably would follow. Many of the Japanese undoubtedly wondered whether their luck, that had seen them through the attack by the

Alden, would last out this time.

Six depth charges slowly sank into the ocean as the corvette passed over the silent Japanese submarine. When the barrels reached their preset depths their charges were fired, igniting the hundreds of pounds of TNT in six massive underwater explosions. Up on the surface, lookouts aboard the *Deloraine* observed huge bursts of bubbles breaking the ocean and patches of oil forming at the surface. Corvette skippers were a thorough bunch, however, and Commander Menlove was not satisfied with an oil slick as evidence of a definite submarine kill, and he ordered the attack to be resumed. The *Deloraine* shot forth all of her remaining depth charges, and two of her sister ships raced up to join in the hunt. USS *Edsall* and *Alden* reappeared at the scene at 7 p.m. The *Edsall*'s sonar operator, Radioman First Class P. W. Hegerfeldt, went immediately to work in assisting the Australian corvettes. 'At 19.29 while searching the area of this attack we picked up a target...range 2,700 yards in Northern edge of the oil slick and separated by approximately ¾ of a mile from the initial target.'[2] Commander J. J. Nix, skipper of the *Edsall*, gave a detailed account of his ship's cooperative effort to confirm the destruction of the Japanese submarine with the *Deloraine*:

> The *EDSALL* changed course...and speed to 5 knots, and sent ranges to the *DELORAINE* informing him that the target was dead ahead. At 1933 the Corvette crossed ahead at a range of 1,500 yards and laid a pattern of depth charges, signalling to the *EDSALL* that he was right over the contact at that time. The *EDSALL* then changed speed to 10 knots, commenced ranging to pick up target. We could not locate the target in the depth charge barrage so crossed middle of barrage at 15 knots...and dropped five depth charges. Two of these charges being set for 150 feet did not go off. Results of both these attacks gave indications that the submarine had been hit; a large amount of oil rising to the surface with air bubbles and evidence of violent disturbances in the water.[3]

The *Deloraine* and the *Edsall* circled like wolves around the disturbed sea, attempting to gain another firm sonar contact. The *Alden* obtained a firm contact at 8 p.m., allowing the *Edsall* to run in at 5 knots and deposit a further six depth charges. Leaving HMAS *Katoomba* and *Lithgow* at the scene the *Deloraine* raced for the supply vessel HMAS *Vigilant* to rearm. Early the following morning, rearming completed, the *Deloraine* arrived back at the scene where the *Katoomba* was still busily depth charging. *Deloraine*'s sonar operator again obtained a contact, often described as most probably the wreck of the *I-124*, and the area was depth charged yet again. Examination of the *Edsall*'s battle report, however, suggests that the *I-124* was still active that morning. Commander Nix notes in his report to the US Asiatic Fleet on 31 January:

> At 0700 on January 21 the *EDSALL* picked up echo bearing 135°, distance 2200 yards, subsequent investigation proved contact had been made with a small submarine; as a maximum of 10° width of target was found at 500 yards distance; at 300 yards propellers were heard.[4]

Further to this evidence of life in the *I-124* on the morning of the 21st, Nix also stated:

> The submarine made violent maneuvers [sic] to lose contact, with the *EDSALL* trailing and attempting to make a good approach.[5]

At 7.50 a.m. the *Edsall* attacked the undoubtedly damaged *I-124*, dropping initially a pattern of six depth charges over the sonar contact. 'Turning hard with full rudder to cross the original line of attack, we dropped only one depth charge. The safety fork from this depth charge dropped into the rack and jammed the rest of the charges in this rack so that they would not release.'[6]

The *Edsall*'s log notes that by 8.32 a.m. the destroyer had joined the two Australian corvettes in continuing to search for the submarine, now also joined by a US Navy PBY Catalina flying boat. By 9 a.m., with no submarine in sight, the *Edsall* had rejoined the *Alden* intending to return to port. The Australian corvettes subsequently reacquired a target and the two American ships stood off while the corvettes plastered the target area. However, at 9.51 a.m. the log records: 'We then examined oil slick at original contact. Seems to be two subs down in this area about ¾ mile apart.'[7] The *Alden* was heading for port low on depth charges, and the Australians were busy bombing the main target, so the *Edsall*, assisted by the circling Catalina, decided to 'hunt this cripple'.[8] However, rain squalls brought the operation to an end by lunchtime, and the *Edsall* returned to port, her captain certain that two Japanese submarines, one large and one small, had been present.

Although a post-war investigation demonstrated that the *Deloraine*'s first attack had probably sunk the *I-124*, the *Katoomba, Lithgow* and *Edsall* were also credited with destroying the Japanese submarine. However, the evidence of Nix's report from the *Edsall* appears to suggest that the *Deloraine* had certainly damaged the *I-124*, but the *Edsall* had been the vessel that had sunk her. The Commander of US Destroyer Squadron 29, of which the *Edsall* was a part, noted rather acerbically in his report of the action to the Commander of US Naval Forces in the south-west Pacific that: 'The Naval Officer in command Darwin was inclined, naturally, to credit the large submarine [sunk] to H.M.A.S. *DELORAINE*.'[9] An inter-service rivalry between the US and Australian navies aside, the end result was the same. The pressure waves created by the depth charge blasts split the *I-124*'s ballast and fuel tanks, knocked out the submarines steering and breached the pressure hull through several blown hatches, that long steel compartmentalized tube housing the eighty-one men clinging to valves, pipes and bits of machinery. High-pressure jets of cold seawater immediately found every opening made through the submarine's fragile hull. Water rapidly filled the compartments which were not closed off with secure hatches, shorting out all the boat's electrics in showers of sparks, killing the lights and the power to the motors. The volume of water flooding the boat rapidly overwhelmed groups of men. As the *I-124* drifted helplessly along the seabed suffocation extinguished the lives of the remaining submariners inside still watertight compartments, trapped forever inside their metal coffin. Commander Menlove of the *Deloraine* was subsequently awarded the Distinguished Service Order for his command of the action and for his sinking of the *I-124*. The Royal Australian Navy conducted an investigation concerning a possible two Japanese submarines noted by many of the ships that took part in the attack on the *I-124*. In the light of insufficient evidence the navy decided that there had only been one target that had moved about on the seabed during the attack, and HMAS *Deloraine* had indeed sunk that target. The wreck of the *I-124* was discovered in 1972, and today it is a protected war grave. A survey conducted by divers from HMAS *Curlew* in 1984 reported that the submarine was intact and upright on the seabed, showing little signs of damage. This has indicated to many enthusiasts that the *I-124*'s pressure hull, or section of the interior of the boat, has remained watertight to the present day and still contains the bodies of the asphyxiated Japanese sailors. HMAS *Deloraine* continued in service, seeing plenty of action off New Guinea in 1944–45, until she was paid off into the Reserve in November 1946. In December 1946 the ship was commissioned once more and worked until 1948 as a minesweeper, clearing up the detritus of war. She was finally paid off in Fremantle in 1948, and ended her days in a breakers yard in Hong Kong in 1956, reduced to scrap.

Staying in the same general operation area as the previous story of the demise of the *I-124*, later in 1942 a Japanese was to earn a ruthless reputation over one particular merchant ship sinking. The Imperial Navy was no more immune from committing outrages against International Law than the army on land. The sinking of the small Burns Philp ship *Mamutu* north of Murray Island in Queensland on 7 August 1942 by the Japanese submarine *RO-33* demonstrated the savagery the Japanese were capable of in war, a savagery directed against innocent women and children.

The Japanese constructed twenty medium submarines of the Kaichu Type, of which the *RO-33* was the first in the series. Four shipyards in Japan built the vessels between 1934 and 1944, the *RO-33* belonging to the earlier K.5 variant. The *RO-33* was 264 feet in length and displaced 1,115 tons. Powered by two diesel engines and a pair of electric motors, the boat had a maximum surface speed of 19.8 knots, or 8 knots submerged. She could travel 5,000 nautical miles at a comfortable 16 knots before refuelling was necessary, making the type ideal for inshore patrol work. By mid-1942 the *RO-33* and her sister vessel, the *RO-34*, were being employed patrolling the waters between New Guinea and Australia, as the Japanese attempted to wrest control of Port Moresby from the Allies.

Fitted with four torpedo tubes, and loaded with just eight torpedoes, the *RO-33* was fitted with a 80mm deck-gun and a 25mm anti-aircraft gun. The Kaichu Type fell victim to massive Allied anti-submarine countermeasures as the war progressed, and of the twenty vessels produced only one, *RO-50*, survived the war to be surrendered to the US Navy. Fifty-four officers and men crewed the type, and the ruthless Lieutenant-Commander Shigeshi Kuriyama, who had taken over the vessel on 18 April 1942, skippered the *RO-33*.

Based at Rabaul, on 20 April *RO-33* departed from the Japanese submarine base to reconnoitre Australian-held Port Moresby in New Guinea. Submarine Division 21 under Captain Hidetoshi Iwagami formed the submarine element of the South Seas Force, the Japanese fleet that was preparing to assist army forces in investing Port Moresby. Submarine Division 21 was ordered to send submarines to reconnoitre the Russell and Deboyne Islands in the hope of discovering useful anchorages before the planned assault began on Port Moresby. The *RO-33* and *RO-34* were then ordered to form a submarine blockade of Port Moresby, to prevent reinforcements and supplies from reaching the embattled Australian troops, and to guide Japanese shipping into the area of operations.

After a brief respite back in Rabaul, the *RO-33* joined Operation Mo, the Japanese invasions of Tulagi, the Solomon Islands and Port Moresby. On 4 May Rear-Admiral Sadamichi Kajioka's Attack Force departed from Rabaul to cover Rear-Admiral Koso Abe's Transport Force taking Japanese troops to attack Port Moresby. Kajioka, aboard the light cruiser *Yubari*, along with four destroyers and a patrol boat, escorted Abe's twelve troop transports. The US Navy's Task Force 17, based around the aircraft carrier USS *Yorktown*, attacked the Tulagi Invasion Force under Rear-Admiral Kiyohide Shima. In what has subsequently become known as the Battle of the Coral Sea, Rear-Admiral Frank J. Fletcher managed to sink a Japanese destroyer and three minesweepers, and damage four other ships, disrupting the Japanese assault. On 5 May the battle widened, as Fletcher's force engaged the Japanese Carrier Strike Force under Vice-Admiral Takeo Takagi. Aircraft from the *Yorktown* and the carrier USS *Lexington* sank the light carrier *Shoho*, but in response Japanese aircraft sank an American destroyer. On the same day the *RO-33* arrived off Port Moresby as the Battle of the Coral Sea grew in ferocity. On 8 May aircraft from the *Lexington* discovered the Japanese carriers *Shokaku* and *Zuikaku*, and *Shokaku* was sufficiently damaged to force her withdrawal from the operation. Although suffering heavy losses, the air group from *Zuikaku* drove home devastating attacks on the *Lexington* and *Yorktown*, resulting in the near destruction of the *Lexington*, which was abandoned and later scuttled.

The Battle of the Coral Sea effectively halted the Japanese central thrust towards Port Moresby, forcing the cancellation of Operation Mo, and the return of the Imperial fleet to Rabaul. Japanese submarines, however, continued harassing operations off the Port Moresby area, and in the waters off northern Queensland in Australia. In the meantime, Port Moresby was under constant Japanese aerial bombardment, some seventy bombing raids being sent against the town by the time the *Mamutu* departed, forcing many of the civilian inhabitants to attempt to flee from New Guinea for the comparative safety of Australia. They would do so by crossing waters aggressively patrolled by Japanese submarines such as the *RO-33*.

On 29 July 1942 the *RO-33* set out from Rabaul to operate in the Coral Sea off Port Moresby and along the south-east coast of New Guinea. The submarine had yet to sink a ship in war, and Commander Kuriyama was undoubtedly determined that this would change. By 6 August the *RO-33* had moved across the Coral Sea north of Murray Island, off the Queensland coast. On the same day the 300-ton *Mamutu*, a white-painted, single smokestack steamer departed the bombed-out ruins of Port Moresby and headed for the small town of Daru, located on the western shores of the Gulf of Papua. From Daru the evacuees could be moved on by ship to Cape York and Australia. Captain McEachern and thirty-seven crewmen had taken aboard eighty-two civilian passengers, including twenty-eight children. The voyage across the Gulf was uneventful until just after 11 a.m. on 7 August when lookouts positioned in the stern spotted a surfaced

Japanese submarine closing in on the vessel. The *Mamutu* was completely unarmed, and McEachern could do little to prevent a Japanese attack, except perhaps hope that the submarine's skipper would not think it prudent to waste a torpedo on such small fry. Commander Kuriyama was of the opinion that expending one of his valuable torpedoes on the *Mamutu* was indeed improvident, but there were other options available to him.

As the *RO-33* rapidly closed with the *Mamutu* Kuriyama ordered the 80mm deck-gun manned and trained on the helpless steamer. Aboard the *Mamutu* considerable panic had broken out, as the civilians aboard realized that the Japanese intended to sink their vessel. The wireless operator had already been instructed to send a Morse code message to Port Moresby advising them of the presence of a Japanese submarine. Any further attempts at communicating with the outside world were abruptly terminated by a Japanese shell that slammed into the radio room, killing the operator instantly and rendering the wireless equipment useless. A second shell soon followed, the bridge exploding outwards in a hail of glass, splintered wood and shrapnel, Captain McEachern dying instantly. The *Mamutu* was now without steering and communications, but heedless of the decks alive with the panicked movement of dozens of crewmen, women and children, the Japanese gunners mercilessly flayed the ship's hull with armour-piercing shells. Many of the passengers were killed or horribly injured as white-hot shards of shrapnel and razor-like pieces of wood and glass cut through the air around them.

Before long the *Mamutu* began to sink, and the dazed and frightened survivors leaped into the water and clung to any floating object they could find, women clutching terrified young children, as the *RO-33* slowed as it came upon them. Survivors noted Japanese sailors running about on the conning tower, long objects being brought up from below, and heard guttural orders bellowed by officers. Some survivors had already begun to swim away from the *RO-33*, realizing instinctively that the danger was not over, when the first rattle of machine-gun fire reached their ears. Japanese sailors atop the conning tower busily worked light machine guns backwards and forwards across the bobbing heads of the *Mamutu*'s dazed survivors, the bullets kicking up plumes of water, as the survivors screams were drowned out by the hail of lead directed towards them. Women and children, some begging for mercy, others screaming in terror, were systematically butchered in this fashion as Kuriyama calmly directed his men's fire. Finally satisfied that the survivors had been disposed of, the *RO-33* motored away from the scene of the crime, leaving a seascape of floating corpses and bits of wreckage soon to be investigated by sharks cruising towards the disturbed underwater sounds that they had sensed, and attracted by the taste of blood in the water. But Kuriyama had not been thorough enough in concealing his crime, for amongst the bodies and wreckage twenty-eight people remained alive, a small fraction of the 120 who had boarded the *Mamutu* the day before. How would they now survive cast adrift in the ocean far from rescue? The answer came in the shape of a B-17 Flying Fortress bomber sent to investigate the *Mamutu*'s report of a Japanese submarine. The B-17 dropped life rafts into the ocean among the survivors, who struggled to board them, and began to make for the shore. In the meantime, word had arrived on Murray Island that a ship was in trouble and the Australian Army signal ship *Reliance* was dispatched to locate the survivors. However, the *Reliance* did not manage to find them, the survivors eventually making their own way to safety.

As for Kuriyama and the *RO-33*, the submarine's days were numbered. After another visit to Rabaul the *RO-33* had been sent back to patrol off Port Moresby. On 29 August it was laying in a submerged position at periscope depth close to the entrance to Port Moresby, when Kuriyama spotted two ships departing the harbour in company. He selected as his target the 3,310-ton merchant ship *Malaita*, which was being escorted by the Royal Australian Navy destroyer HMAS *Arunta*. Both ships were sailing to Cairns to escape the incessant Japanese bombing raids on Port Moresby. At 11.34 a.m. the *Malaita* was struck by a single torpedo on her starboard side below the bridge, and the freighter heeled over immediately, taking on a heavy list. The captain gave the order to abandon ship at 12.45 p.m., as he feared the vessel was about to capsize completely, but the list was eventually arrested, and the crew re-boarded her. The *Malaita* would survive her encounter with the *RO-33*, and was taken in tow back to Port

Moresby. The *RO-33*, however, was not so lucky. The *Arunta* had begun an immediate Asdic search for the submarine, and was not slow in locating a promising submerged target. Commander J. C. Morrow aboard the *Arunta* ordered several depth charge attacks launched over the Asdic target, eventually resulting in large quantities of fuel oil rising to the surface. Entombed in their shattered steel coffin on the bottom of the Coral Sea lay Kuriyama and his fifty-three subordinates, a fittingly gruesome end for a murderous and sadistic commander and crew.

Notes

1. *Commanding Officer to Commander in Chief, US Asiatic Fleet, Action taken against Submarines by USS* Edsall, *January 31, 1942* (Film Nix, DK, National Archives [NARA], Washington DC.)
2. ibid.
3. ibid.
4. ibid.
5. ibid
6. ibid.
7. *Confidential Action Report. Activities of USS* Edsall *for January 20–21 [Covers anti-submarine operations while escorting "Trinity" to Port Darwin, Australia.], 22 January 1942*, (Film Nix, DK, National Archives [NARA], Washington DC.)
8. ibid.
9. *Commander Destroyer Squadron Twenty-Nine to The Commander, U.S. Naval Forces Southwest Pacific, 1st Endorsement on CO* EDSALL, *February 10, 1942*, (Film Nix, DK, National Archives [NARA], Washington DC.

Chapter 5

Bombarding America

...the broad oceans that have been heralded in the past as our protection from attack have become endless battlefields on which we are constantly being challenged by our enemies.

President Franklin D. Roosevelt, 23 February 1942

Sensible Americans know that the submarine shelling of the Pacific coast was a warning to the nation that the Paradise created by George Washington is on the verge of destruction.

Radio Tokyo, 3 March 1942

Following the attacks launched on American coastal shipping along the west coast of the United States during December 1941, one of the submarines involved was probably responsible for sparking an invasion scare in America. The *I-17*, under Lieutenant-Commander Kozo Nishino, moved to complete the original orders issued to all nine Japanese submarine skippers on entering United States waters. As related in Chapter 2, the Imperial Navy's 6th Fleet at Kwajalein had conceived a two-part plan. Vice-Admiral Shimizu had ordered the submarines to interdict American merchant shipping, and then to expend remaining deck-gun ammunition against shore targets. The submarines *I-17, I-19, I-21* and *I-23* had all launched deck-gun and torpedo attacks against American coastal merchantmen, with hardly any successes. The *I-17* had attacked the *Samoa* on 18 December, and had failed to sink her. On 20 December Nishino had attacked the *Emidio*, and although he had inflicted damage the ship did not sink and the abandoned vessel had eventually run aground. The *I-23* had attacked the tanker *Agwiworld*, also on 20 December, but had failed to sink her. The *I-21* engaged the *H.*

M. Story on 22 December, but the pattern had repeated itself and the ship had escaped further attention. On the following day the *I-21* had intercepted yet another tanker, the *Larry Doheny*, but the vessel fortunately escaped the Japanese submarine's clutches, leading to deep frustration among the submarine's crew. Commander Matsumura tried again shortly after, and this time did manage to sink the tanker *Montebello*, as well as attempting to massacre the surviving crewmembers in complete violation of International Law, and the treaties and protocols Japan had herself signed before the war. The *I-19*, however, had had very little success, missing the schooner *Barbara Olsen* with a torpedo on 24 December, and damaging the freighter *Absaroka* later that same day. The *Absaroka* was run aground and subsequently survived.

Several reasons for the apparent inability of Japanese submarines to sink unarmed and unescorted American merchant vessels can be suggested. Firstly there is the issue of tactics. Attempting to shell a ship using the submarine's deck-gun began many of the attacks. Unfavourable sea conditions and poor light cruelly exposed the ineffectiveness of this strategy, as many of the attacks were made at night, or in the very early morning. Secondly, the torpedo attacks launched by the submarines were no less fraught with failure. The powerful Long Lance torpedo either missed the target through human error, or passed beneath the target due to bad luck. When they did strike they often caused insufficient damage to sink the target vessel immediately. The Japanese submarine skippers appeared to be labouring under an official order requesting them to expend only one torpedo per merchant ship attacked. This was a limiting factor on a submariner's ability to use the torpedo to its full potential as a weapon, especially as compared with the German (and that of the British and American) tactic of firing a spread or two or more torpedoes at a target to better ensure a hit and the destruction of the targeted vessel. A third factor that appeared to limit the success of the Japanese submarine campaign along America's west coast was the fledgling American anti-submarine forces ranged against the Japanese. Although in their infancy in terms of experience and technology, these aircraft and warships managed to disrupt some of the Japanese submarine attacks, and to deter

Japanese skippers from following through with their attacks. Although the Japanese Navy's chief of staff, Admiral Nagano, cancelled the order he had issued to submarines to bombard shore targets in America, as he feared retaliatory attacks on Japanese installations and towns, Commander Nishino in the *I-17* appears to have ignored his orders and to have proceeded with the original instructions to strike the shore.

The story of Nishino's attack on the Barnsdall Oil Company's Ellwood refinery located ten miles north of Santa Barbara, California, appears rooted simply in a desire for personal revenge. During the late 1930s Nishino was a merchant seaman, captain of a Japanese oil tanker that had arrived at the Ellwood refinery's mile-long row of derricks for unloading. Oil company executives invited Nishino and his crew to a welcoming ceremony north of the beach. As Nishino and his men made their way along a path from the beach the proud Japanese sea captain slipped, and landed on top of a prickly-pear cactus. Delighted American oil workers could not control themselves at the sight of Captain Nishino having cactus spines extracted from his backside, and Nishino's humiliation and loss of face was complete. It must also be remembered that in February 1942 Japan stood at the high water mark of her conquests. British Malaya had fallen, and the great naval base of Singapore had surrendered to the Japanese on 15 February, and 100,000 British, Australian and Indian troops had fallen into Japanese hands. In Burma, the British were in retreat, conducting a fighting withdrawal through a thousand miles of hills and jungle. The 17th Indian Division was, by February, in serious danger of being cut off at the Sittang River, the British exit into the relative safety of India. The war was also going badly for the United States. General Douglas MacArthur's forces were bottled up in the Bataan Peninsula on the island of Luzon in the Philippines, and MacArthur himself had just been ordered to abandon his doomed command by no less than President Franklin Roosevelt himself and flee ignominiously to Australia. The American island of Wake had been in Japanese hands for two months, and fast approaching it were the remnants of the US Pacific Fleet, a small task force built around the carrier USS *Enterprise* commanded by Admiral William 'Bull' Halsey. The Japanese were poised to launch an invasion of Java in the

Netherlands East Indies, one of the final frontiers of Allied resistance in the south before Australia.[1] Perhaps personal reasons drove Nishino to disregard Nagano's orders and shell the American coast, and perhaps his decision was made in a moment of national euphoria, as the expanding Japanese empire appeared unstoppable. After later battlefield reverses some Japanese military officers were to label this total belief in the abilities of the military to continue their conquests the 'victory disease'.

By February 1942 Nishino had returned to the area of his humiliation several years before, but this time commanding a well-armed and powerful submarine. On the evening of 23 February, as the light disappeared from the sky, the Japanese submarine motored on the surface towards the giant refinery, its dozens of derricks fronting huge aviation fuel storage tanks situated on a hill behind the beach. Nishino stood on the conning tower bridge, scanning the place he hated more than perhaps any other with binoculars, the deck-gunners having already loaded their weapon with a 140mm shell. At exactly 7.15 p.m. Nishino ordered the gunners to commence firing. The first reports of the gun, which echoed across the mile or so of sea separating the submarine from the land, brought local residents and oil workers to their windows. Many workers rushed out of a popular local drinking hole where they were relaxing after a hard day of labour. Confusion reigned after the impact of the first shell as people attempted to locate the source of the explosion. As the deck-gun banged out for a second time oil workers spotted the Japanese submarine sitting on the surface out at sea opposite the refinery, workman G.O. Brown commenting afterwards that it was 'so big I thought it might be a destroyer or a cruiser'. Within minutes the local police were informed of an enemy submarine boldly sitting on the surface, firing at the oil refinery. The local sheriff assured the callers that American aircraft were on their way to deal with the intruder. However, the American authorities would be unable to do very much about it, a fact not lost on Commander Nishino.

Anywhere between sixteen and twenty-four shells were fired by the *I-17*; accounts vary. Eleven were counted falling into the sea, while at least three struck and damaged rigging and pumping equipment at an oil head. Other shells passed over the refinery to land on ranches up to three miles from the coast. Nishino certainly came close to starting a major conflagration, as one shell exploded in a field only thirty yards from one of the giant aviation storage tanks. Suddenly, Nishino abruptly ordered the gunners to cease firing at 7.35 p.m., and the *I-17* departed the scene on the surface, moving along the Santa Barbara Channel for the open sea. At the small town of Montecito, sixteen miles east of Ellwood, Reverend Arthur Basham noticed the submarine '...heading south toward Los Angeles and flashing lights as if it were attempting to signal with the shore'. The submarine was still reported to be motoring on the surface at 8.30 p.m. by coastal residents, and Basham's report to local police fuelled suspicions that Japanese-Americans had been in communication with Nishino's boat and aided his locating targets. Reports of flashing lights out at sea off Santa Barbara led to the imposition of a blackout until just after midnight as local authorities feared further bombardments against shore communities.

Nishino's attack, though perhaps only serving as one man's lust for revenge, cannot be entirely dismissed as a freak event. The huge Ellwood oil refinery was an important military and economic target, and had Nishino succeeded in setting fire to the aviation fuel stored there, he would have scored a significant victory. Commander Nishino made history by becoming the first person to successfully attack the mainland of the United States since the War of 1812. But, more important by far was the fear and panic Nishino's audacious attack sparked off along the American west coast. Many believed the United States was about to be invaded, coming so soon on the back of the successful Japanese attack on Pearl Harbor only three months before. What occurred in Los Angeles just days after the Ellwood refinery attack demonstrated to everyone that invasion fears were widespread and all that was required was a spark to ignite the entire coastal region.

Following the *I-17*'s successful deck-gun bombardment of the Ellwood Oil Refinery on 23 February, United States forces defending the west coast were placed on high alert. Another scenario apart from invasion faced by the United States authorities was a Japanese air raid on one or more of the large west coast metropolises such as Seattle, San Francisco, Los Angeles and San Diego. It was not beyond the realms of possibility that a Japanese carrier force could repeat the kind of mass aerial attack witnessed at Pearl Harbor, this time attempting to disrupt civilian life instead of destroying a military target (not forgetting that all of these cities had a sizeable US Navy presence). Nishino's attack further undermined relations between white and Japanese-Americans, which had already been severely eroded following the Pearl Harbor raid.

In Los Angeles, anti-aircraft guns and searchlights were standing ready to take on the Japanese, an alert system was operational with 10,000 air raid wardens ready to take to the streets, and army radar units carefully monitored their green scopes for a Japanese presence in the skies above the 'City of Angels'. At 2.25 a.m. on 25 February, as most residents of Los Angeles slept soundly in their beds, an eerie sound grew across the city heralding imminent danger.[2] Hundreds of air raid sirens wailed through the still night air, triggered by the spark necessary to light the invasion fear touch paper – a radar contact recorded at slightly before 2 a.m. The blip on the radar screen was formally identified at 2.07 a.m. as an unidentified aircraft approaching the coast. Officers at IV Interceptor Command, tasked with defending Los Angeles from aerial attack, immediately posted a yellow alert. For fifteen minutes the unknown contact was tracked, still approaching Los Angeles, and as the aircraft did not deviate from its course the alert status was upgraded to blue. A blue alert signified to military, civil defence and police authorities that the aircraft was presumed to be hostile. Following just three minutes later was the order to go to the red alert status. As far as the authorities were now concerned, an enemy air raid was imminent. Across the city the mournful blaring of air raid sirens awakened residents. Searchlight beams stabbed out into the night sky, the city was blacked-out, and anti-aircraft batteries reported themselves 'manned-and-ready' to IV Interceptor Command Headquarters. Thousands of air raid wardens and police officers took to the streets to assist the military.

By 2.32 a.m. all anti-aircraft batteries and searchlight units had completed reporting their status.[3] The anti-aircraft weapons employed by IV Interceptor Command were 37mm cannon and larger 3-inch guns. The combined number of guns within Los Angeles could place forty-eight flak shells into the sky every minute, creating a perilous curtain of fire for any would-be bombers to penetrate. At 3.16 a.m. all anti-aircraft guns suddenly commenced firing, hundreds of shells exploding like some crazed fireworks display high above the city, until the guns ceased firing at 3.36 a.m. Searchlights continued to trace bright patterns across the sky, when suddenly, at 4.05 a.m. the flak guns recommenced firing. At 4.15 a.m. silence once more returned to the city as the batteries ceased their blind hammering of the empty sky. Thirty minutes of sustained anti-aircraft fire had hurled approximately 1,440 rounds of both 37mm and 3-inch ammunition into the air above Los Angeles, equating to a massive ten tons of ordnance.[4] Most of the shells had exploded at their preset altitudes, some had not. Either way, ten tons of expended shrapnel and unexploded shells now fell back onto the city below. Some of the larger 3-inch shells that had failed to explode in mid-air detonated instead when they began impacting all over Los Angeles. Houses and garages were damaged, as white-hot shards of shrapnel ripped through homes, often narrowly missing terrified residents.

As the sun came up later that morning army bomb disposal teams were at work all over the city, roping off streets from curious bystanders before making safe American 3-inch shells that had buried themselves in roads and gardens without exploding. Incredibly, only eight citizens of Los Angeles had died during the 'air raid', most from heart attacks or accidents in the blackout. At the North American Aviation factory complex located at Inglewood, brand-new B-25 Mitchell medium bombers were discovered with wings peppered by falling shrapnel. More serious was the metaphorical fallout of the 'air raid' in the treatment of California's Japanese-American community. Several days prior to the phantom raid on Los Angeles, President Roosevelt had issued Executive Order 9066. This law required the enforced internment of all Japanese-Americans for the duration of the conflict in 'concentration camps' outside the city. During the night of the 'air raid' police, who believed them to have been signalling to enemy aircraft with lights, arbitrarily arrested dozens of Japanese-Americans. Most of these people were only guilty of driving a car during a blackout, or other minor infractions of the law.

The questions began almost as soon as the last flak shell

dropped back onto the city: did the Japanese attack Los Angeles on 25 February 1942? The answer is an emphatic 'no'. Reporters arrived at a ludicrous figure of fifty enemy aircraft over the city during the 'air raid', and the American military provided some face-saving 'evidence' with which to prove that an attack had indeed taken place. For example, the 122nd Coast Artillery Regiment, guarding an aircraft factory at Downey, identified several aircraft flying beyond the maximum range of their guns, but fired at them anyway. At Long Beach, Battery G, 78th Coast Artillery Regiment protecting the Douglas Aircraft factory, logged twenty-five to thirty enemy bombers, followed half an hour later by another fifteen, all flying in formation. This battery fired 246 3-inch shells into the sky, claiming the mystery bombers then moved out to sea.[5] Officially at least, the Japanese did launch an attack on Los Angeles, according to the US Army after receiving several reports from anti-aircraft batteries. The army settled on a tentative estimate of fifteen enemy aircraft over the city between 2.30 a.m. and 4.30 a.m. This raises an obvious question: fifteen aircraft could only have come from a Japanese aircraft carrier, and a detailed search undertaken the next day failed to demonstrate a Japanese naval presence in inshore west coast waters (submarines not included). In the light of this news the authorities changed their official story, stating that the fifteen aircraft reported were most probably of civilian origin, and had been, conveniently, piloted by enemy agents. On 26 February, the Secretary of the Navy, Frank Knox, completely undermined the army's statements when he declared that the 'air raid' on Los Angeles had been a false alarm. The US Army continued to defend its original assertion for some time, eventually requiring Congressional intervention, perhaps unwilling to accept the embarrassment of having been firing at phantoms rather than Japanese bombers on the night of 25 February. No evidence has ever been produced to prove that the Japanese did raid Los Angeles, no bomb damage was recorded anywhere in the city, no planes were downed by anti-aircraft fire, and no one has ever come forward to say that they participated in the raid, Japanese pilot or 'enemy agent'. The reaction of IV Interceptor Command to the unidentified aircraft that appeared on their radar screens was perhaps indicative of how all citizens of the west coast felt and wanted to react after the *I-17* attack. Clearly, the Americans were seeing Japanese aircraft where there were none. Japanese submarines were very real, however, and all Americans living in California and Oregon knew that the enemy was close. What the phantom Los Angeles air raid perhaps demonstrated above all else was the fears of invasion and attack Americans were living with in early 1942, and the competence of the civil defence and anti-aircraft units whose job was to protect the city. They did their job on the night of 25 February, and stood ready to protect the city from any future Japanese attack.

Commander Nishino and the *I-17* remained at their assigned patrol area after the attack on the Ellwood Oil Refinery. On 28 February, five days after the shore bombardment, and three following the phantom Japanese air raid on Los Angeles, Nishino struck again. Lookouts located the tanker *William A. Berg*, and Nishino shot a single torpedo at the American ship.[6] Fortunately for the merchant seamen the Japanese torpedo detonated prematurely, but Nishino believed that he had struck the tanker. The *William A. Berg* escaped damage and made off from the scene of her close brush with disaster.

Less than three months after the gigantic Japanese aerial and submarine onslaught against Pearl Harbor a second, considerably more modest, raid on the US Pacific Fleet's anchorage was mounted by the Imperial Navy. Although nothing more than a 'nuisance raid', the logistical planning required to strike once again at American soil demonstrated the excellent Japanese use of aircraft and submarines working in close cooperation. Submarines were destined to play a crucial role in the operation, codenamed 'K', and much more effectively than the suicidal midget submarine attacks of December 1941.

The Japanese devised a plan to use a pair of newly introduced Kawanishi H8K1 four-engine naval flying boats of the 24th Air Flotilla to strike Oahu.[7] These aircraft, given the codename 'Emily' by the Allies, had a maximum range of 3,040 miles and were able to haul one ton of bombs. They were a Japanese equivalent of the famous British Short Sunderland, though larger (incidentally, before the war the Kawanishi company had had a close working partnership with Belfast-based seaplane manufacturers Short Brothers). The plan would see both of these huge aircraft, each with a crew of ten, fly from a starting point at Wotje Atoll in the Marshall Islands to a midway point and rendezvous position at the remote French Frigate Shoals located 482 miles from Pearl Harbor. The submarine *I-9* was 'assigned to take up station midway between Wotje and the Shoal and act as a radio beacon'[8] for the two flying boats. At French Frigate Shoals the pair of flying boats would meet two large Japanese submarines that would be waiting for them inside the protected lagoon. The two submarines selected for the primary part of the mission were the *I-15* and *I-19* respectively, both boats normally being fitted with the tiny two-seater Yokosuka E14Y1 floatplane for reconnaissance in a watertight hanger in front of the conning tower. For the purposes of Operation K the planes were removed and replaced with ten tons of aviation fuel in drums on each submarine, packed inside the hangar space for safe transit to French Frigate Shoals. After the arrival of the flying boats the two submarines would replenish the planes' fuel tanks before the Kawanishi's set off on the final leg of their outbound mission to Oahu. As a backup, should either of the two submarines be lost, the *I-26* was directed to shadow the pair and act as a reserve fuel tanker, and also to act as a picket to constantly scan for any enemy activity in the vicinity.

The submarine *I-23*, under Lieutenant-Commander Genichi Shibata, had a more hazardous task to perform, which required her to creep as close as ten miles from the coast of Oahu and report on weather conditions over the target. Additionally, should either or both of the flying boats be shot down during the run over Pearl Harbor, the *I-23* was to attempt to rescue any downed aircrew.

The Kawanishi H8K1 was also nicknamed the 'Flying Porcupine', and for good reason. Mounted in turrets and blisters around the aircraft were five 20mm cannon and four 7.7mm machine guns, making it a dangerous quarry for any roving Allied fighter to tackle. A pair working in close cooperation, and covering one another with their guns would be more concerned about ground anti-aircraft fire than fighter interception.

The Japanese selected 1 March 1942 as the day of the attack, and all submarines taking part in the operation were expected to be in position one day before the flying boats showed up. The *I-15* and *I-19* sailed imperiously into the lagoon at French Frigate Shoals at the assigned time, deck-guns fully manned in case American lookouts or coast watchers had been planted on the islands. Lieutenant Toshi Hashizume and Ensign Tomaro had been selected as the pilots of the respective Kawanishi's, and they departed from Yokosuka harbour in Japan on 15 February and began the long journey to the mission jumping-off point. The flight plan took them first to Saipan in the Marianas, then the big Japanese naval base at Truk in the Carolines, and on to Jaliut in the Marshall Islands before they splashed down at Wotje Atoll. Weather was the all-important factor determining when the mission actually began, and information about the weather over Oahu came to the Japanese from two different sources. Firstly, they had cleverly cracked the local weather reporting code used by US naval air stations at Midway Island, Hawaii and Johnson Atoll. The second source would come from the submarine *I-23*, positioned ten miles to the south of Oahu. Unfortunately, just as the Japanese were gearing up to launch the mission all information concerning weather ceased. Two things had occurred which meant a delay in launching the aircraft on their way to Pearl Harbor. The first was a routine change in the code being used by the US Navy to report weather conditions over their airfields in the region, leaving the Japanese outside of the information loop. The other was the sudden loss of contact with the *I-23*. Radio communications emanating from the Japanese were also being picked up by the Americans, indicating to them that there was Japanese submarine activity in the area of French Frigate Shoals, '...so the Americans, centered on the Naval Combat Intelligence Unit at Pearl Harbor, broke Japanese naval codes, enabling them to ascertain the whereabouts of Japanese surface and submarine assets'.[9] The sudden loss of contact with the *I-23* was ominous, and, according to Hackett and Kingsepp, the Japanese Navy presumed the submarine lost with all hands on 28 February off Hawaii.

One of the principal Japanese naval bases in the Western Pacific, located at Rabaul in New Britain, now found itself menaced by an American naval task force that was discovered to be steaming towards the base as weather reports ceased, and the mission began to look in doubt. The task force, built around the aircraft carrier USS *Lexington*, appeared a juicy target to the Imperial Fleet's local headquarters at Truk, and all available submarines and surface warships headed out and searched for the force. The two days spent on attempting to locate and attack the American task force, which aborted a projected attack on Rabaul, meant that the Pearl Harbor raid itself was delayed until 3 March. In the early evening the two big flying boats touched down safely in the lagoon at French Frigate Shoals, and the crews of the *I-15* and *I-19* set to work refuelling the huge beasts. At 9.38 p.m., both aircraft had lifted off and turned towards Pearl Harbor, the crews readying themselves for the daring strike against a location still clearing up the detritus and wreckage from the first Japanese raid, and a place maintaining a much better surveillance of the skies and seas around Hawaii, determined not to be caught out again by a sudden 'surprise' attack.

US Navy intelligence officers had spent the remainder of 3 March pondering the significance of Japanese submarine activity at French Frigate Shoals that had arrived on their desks from the decrypts of Imperial Navy radio communications. The officers remained unsure as to what it signified, and more importantly, whether such activity posed a threat to local American forces. The massive raid of 7 December 1941 against Pearl Harbor had been launched from Japanese aircraft carriers, and none were believed to be near to Hawaii in March 1942. No land-based Japanese aircraft had the range to reach Hawaii from the furthest regions of the Japanese Empire, and although the officers were aware that some of the larger Japanese submarines certainly mounted a small plane onboard, they also knew that the aircraft was essentially a harmless reconnaissance model that they had codenamed 'Glen'. For the moment, the reports of enemy submarine activity remained routine, and no alarms were raised or the alert status at Pearl Harbor brought up a notch.

The pair of Kawanishi flying boats continued to devour the miles between the Shoals and a blacked-out Oahu, oblivious to the radar beams that constantly scanned the skies around the Hawaiian Islands. A US Army radar station at Kauai was the first section of the airborne early warning system to record a possible problem. At 12.14 a.m. on 4 March the radar 'painted' a single target moving towards Oahu at a range of 240 miles. The soldiers immediately informed the Air Raid Defense Center, who in turn telephoned the local Army Air Corps and US Navy air stations throughout the islands requesting that any friendly aircraft airborne be reported to the centre, and so could be eliminated from the air defence equation. Both the army and the navy replied that they had no aircraft then airborne, so the unidentified radar target was deemed most likely hostile.

Unlike on the morning of 7 December 1941, this time the Americans responded quickly and efficiently to the threat they now perceived to be fast approaching. At 12.43 a.m. the air defence commander ordered general quarters, bringing all military and civil defence personnel to full readiness of an impending air raid on Oahu. At 1.15 a.m. a trio of US Navy PBY Catalina flying boats took off with orders to seek out any Japanese aircraft carriers lurking close to the islands that would explain the presence of enemy aircraft bearing down on Pearl Harbor. Four Curtiss P-40 Warhawks formed local air defence, and these fighters were scrambled at 1.36 a.m. to form a Combat Air Patrol (CAP) over Pearl Harbor with orders to intercept and shoot down any hostile aircraft encountered. This was easier said than done, as the Americans lacked any dedicated night fighters, and as the P-40s were bereft of radar the pilots would have to hunt by following ground directions and using their eyes. Although originally the night had been clear, with a full, bright moon, the weather had rapidly deteriorated, and rain and clouds were now building up over the intended Japanese target. The rain that would prevent the P-40s from discovering the Japanese flying boats that night also prevented the two amphibious bombers from satisfactorily locating their targets.

The two pilots, Hashizume and Tomaro, planned to deposit their bombs over the central Ten-Ten Dock at Pearl Harbor, but as the two Japanese planes made landfall at the extreme western tip of Oahu and headed inland across the Koolau Mountains at 15,000 feet, both pilots noticed the clouds and rain squalls building up ahead of their machines. The Japanese planes stuck to an easterly course that would take them to the north of Pearl Harbor. Once close to the harbour the amphibians would make a sharp turn to port and head south to begin their bombing runs over the base. Lieutenant Hashizume's aircraft followed the set course and arrived over the harbour as planned, but the target was badly obscured by cloud cover. Some members of his crew yelled over the intercom that they had seen Ford Island in the centre of the Pearl Harbor naval base through breaks in the cloud, but Hashizume decided to fly on, make a turn, and come back for a second look before releasing his bombs. The pilot banked the huge aircraft round to port and started back for his bomb run, dropping his payload at 12.10 a.m. through the clouds. These bombs rained down on some trees carpeting the slopes of Mount Tantalus behind Honolulu, six miles from Pearl Harbor. Four booming explosions echoed off the hills to mark the arrival of the Japanese, though hardly a soul registered the detonations as having a Japanese origin.

The second aircraft, with Ensign Tomaro at the controls, did no better than Hashizume. When Hashizume had made his sharp turn to port designed to bring him back over the target, Tomaro had misunderstood Hashizume's order and had carried on following the southern route. Realizing his mistake with the disappearance of his wingman, Tomaro hauled the big flying boat around and retraced his path back north. At 12.30 a.m., unsure of his exact position but believing himself to be over Pearl Harbor, Tomaro released his bombs, which fell harmlessly into the sea. Both Kawanishi's now formed up and headed away from the islands with all possible haste, leaving the P-40s and Catalinas to search fruitlessly for them.

Hashizume's aircraft had completed the mission with a punctured hull, and this aircraft headed straight for Jaluit for repairs. Tomaro took his plane to Wotje Atoll, arriving at 2.45 p.m. Both pilots wrote detailed reports of their sorties over Oahu, and both men concluded correctly that the level of damage they had inflicted on the naval base was difficult to determine, owing to the weather conditions they had encountered over the target. Back at Pearl Harbor, to begin with the four explosions that had been heard on Mount Tantalus were investigated. The Americans initially thought that one of their own aircraft from either the army or the navy had dumped its bomb load in the countryside before landing, but closer examination of bomb fragments recovered from the scene revealed them to be of Japanese manufacture. An even more extraordinary answer to the riddle of how the Japanese had carried out the daring long distance attack slowly revealed itself, an interesting case of life imitating art.

American intelligence had suppressed a short story written by a serving naval officer in 1940 entitled *Rendezvous*.[10] The story, by W.J. Holmes, then a lieutenant, told of a fictional American raid on a Japanese base. In the story, the Americans plan to bomb Japanese preparations for an amphibious operation by using flying boats. Because the flying boats lack the range to reach Japan from Hawaii, three submarines are used to refuel the aircraft at the fictional 'Moab Atoll' located 1,000 miles from Japan. The American submarines carried not only aviation fuel for the thirsty flying boats, but the bombs that they would drop on the mythical port of 'Bosoko' in the raid. The Office of Naval Intelligence had suppressed the story in November 1940, but after Holmes defended his right to publish using examples of similar British and Italian seaplane operations, the navy relented and *Rendezvous* appeared in the August 1941 edition of the *Saturday Evening Post*. Following the Japanese raid on Pearl Harbor in March 1942, Rear-Admiral Edwin Layton, chief intelligence officer to the commander-in-chief of the US Pacific Fleet, Admiral Chester W. Nimitz, disclosed that the Japanese had most probably copied the idea for the raid from Holmes's short story, supplanting 'Moab Atoll' for the very real French Frigate Shoals as a refuelling waypoint. In the story *Rendezvous* the Americans manage to wreck the Japanese ships assembling in 'Bosoko' harbour for an amphibious attack. In the real mission, the Japanese failed to cause any damage, apart from digging up some trees.

The Americans looked carefully at Holmes's story, and decided in light of the recent attack to dispatch the destroyer USS *Ballard* to the French Frigate Shoals to take a careful look, and leave behind some mines should any Japanese submarines have returned. They never did, and the evident failure of so complex an operation, including the use of three fleet submarines that would have been better employed elsewhere, meant that the Japanese would not attempt another operation of this sort again.

The Junsen Type-B submarine *I-26* had an interesting claim to fame. On 7 December 1941, as Imperial Navy aircraft and midget submarines struck the US Pacific Fleet at Pearl Harbor the *I-26* was hunting a thousand miles north-east of Honolulu. It was here that Lieutenant-Commander Minoru Yokota found and sank the *Cynthia Olson*, an American merchant ship on her way from Tacoma, Washington to Honolulu. In Hawaii a shore station registered a distress signal from the vessel, reporting that a submarine was attacking her. Of the thirty-five crewmen aboard the vessel, none survived. The *Cynthia Olson* was the first American merchant ship sunk by a Japanese submarine in the Second World War. On 11 December, also in the waters around Hawaii, the *I-9* under Lieutenant-Commander Fujii discovered the American freighter *Lahaina*. The vessel was sunk 800 miles off Honolulu, and four men died either during the sinking or from exposure during ten days spent at sea in lifeboats before the crewmen were washed ashore at Kahtilui on the island of Maui.

The *I-26* had spent the remainder of 1941 and early 1942 patrolling off the Strait of Juan de Fuca, a major arterial waterway serving the port of Seattle. By June 1942 the *I-26* was still lurking off the entrance to the Strait, thirty-five miles south-west of Cape Flattery. On Sunday 7 June the 3,286-ton American freighter *Coast Trader* was sailing from Port Angeles bound for San Francisco, the crew unaware that a large Japanese submarine had been trailing them in their wake since they had turned south on leaving the Strait. The Japanese were observing every movement of the freighter and preparing to mount an attack.

The ironically named Submarine Boat Company of Edison, New Jersey had constructed the *Coast Trader* in 1920. Originally the vessel was named the *Point Reyes*, and after fitting out, the 324-foot long freighter had gone to work for the US Shipping Board. In 1936 the Coastwise Line Steamship Company had purchased the *Point Reyes* from the government, renamed her the *Coast Trader*, and had made Portland, Oregon her new homeport. When America had entered the Second World War the *Coast Trader* had been placed under indefinite charter to the US Army. To this end she carried aboard her nineteen American soldiers forming an 'Armed Guard' unit tasked with defending the ship from enemy attack.[11]

On 7 June the *Coast Trader* was steaming south down the coast loaded with 1,250-tons of newsprint, arranged in bundles of paper each weighing 2,000 pounds. Captain Lyle G. Havens was fully aware that since December 1941 Japanese submarines had been preying on unescorted American merchant ships plying the west coast inshore trade routes. Havens had posted lookouts fore and aft with orders to keep a sharp watch on the sea for signs of submarines. What these lookouts failed to detect was the periscope of the *I-26* cutting through the water aft of the *Coast Trader*, a baleful glass eye sizing up its victim. The *I-26*, at 356.5 feet in length, was also much larger than the *Coast Trader*.

Commander Yokota had decided to launch a submerged torpedo attack, abandoning earlier tactics that had involved Japanese submarines in deck-gun bombardments of merchant ships, and occasional surfaced torpedo attacks. The *Coast Trader* was unaware of the presence of the *I-26* until a Long Lance torpedo ploughed through the stern hull plates on the starboard side and detonated within the ship. The hatch covers over the holds were blown open and several tons of burning baled newsprint sailed into the sky to scatter in the sea around the stricken ship. The *Coast Trader*'s engines had been stopped by the impact of the torpedo. In the radio shack the operator desperately attempted to call for assistance, but both the main mast and the radio antenna had been felled by the torpedo's explosion, and this rendered communication with the shore impossible. After quickly assessing the situation and receiving damage reports Captain Havens concluded that his ship was done for and gave the order to abandon her. Launching the ship's two lifeboats proved to be difficult. The torpedo had cracked the *Coast Trader*'s refrigeration system releasing poisonous ammonia fumes that caused the crew some problems. Men were forced to lie down on the deck to recover. The starboard lifeboat had also been damaged, and it was decided that it would have to be abandoned. This meant that only the port side lifeboat and two large cork rafts were available to take off the fifty-six members of the crew. In an orderly fashion the crew abandoned the *Coast Trader*, launching their craft onto a calm sea. Some of the crew observed the partly submerged conning tower of the *I-26* hovering like a shark's dorsal fin on the water's surface barely 200 yards from the foundering ship. Commander Yokota had decided to remain submerged, monitoring the death of the *Coast Trader* through his periscope. He did not have long to wait. At 2.50 p.m. the *Coast Trader* sank by the stern and the *I-26* quietly departed from the scene, commander and crew eminently satisfied with their day's work.

For the crew of the *Coast Trader* their problems were only just beginning. As the *I-26* motored away rain began to fall. Captain Havens realized that they must remain together and he had the lifeboat and the two rafts secured to each other with lengths of rope. Several crewmen had been injured during the Japanese attack, and Havens now had all the injured transferred to the more seaworthy lifeboat. The skipper now decided that because of the damage inflicted on the communications equipment aboard the *Coast Trader* he could assume that no distress signal had been received onshore. Therefore, it would be up to the crew themselves to save themselves. Havens and the survivors observed the deteriorating sea conditions, as a great howling wind came up and the waves grew steeper. The skipper ordered the lifeboat crew to begin rowing towards the shore, towing the two attached cork rafts loaded with the remainder of the crew. Towards midnight the lines securing the rafts to the lifeboat parted company, and the lifeboat was unable to force its way back through the high seas to replace the umbilical. Captain Havens ordered his men to resume pulling for the shore. As the dawn came the heavy seas and high wind began to abate, and this enabled a small sail to be rigged on the lifeboat. All morning and through most of the afternoon of the 8 June the survivors rowed and sailed their flimsy craft towards land, always aware that over half of the crew of the *Coast Trader* remained trapped on rafts adrift at the mercy of the sea. At approximately 4 p.m. the exhausted survivors spotted another vessel on the horizon and began pulling towards it with their last ounces of energy. The ship was the *Virginia I*, a fishing boat based in San Francisco out trawling for halibut. The survivors from the lifeboat were immediately taken to a US Navy post at Neah Bay. The navy launched a coordinated effort to find and rescue the men left on the two cork rafts. These men had to spend another night at sea, as US Coast Guard aircraft began a search and rescue operation. The men on the two rafts sighted one of the searching planes slightly before dawn on Tuesday 9 June, an officer from the *Coast Trader* firing an orange signal flare into the sky to alert the pilot. The Coast Guard aircraft immediately radioed the position of the life rafts in to the US Navy, who passed on this information to the nearest Allied ship in the vicinity – the Royal Canadian Navy corvette HMCS *Edmunston*. The Canadian warship raced to the scene, and after enduring forty hours on open rafts, battered by cold seas, high winds and rain the exhausted survivors were hauled aboard. The *Edmunston* immediately made for Port Angeles to offload the remaining crew of the *Coast Trader*.[12]

Many of the crew of the *Coast Trader* required hospitalization for the injuries they had sustained as a result of the Japanese attack, or because they were suffering from exposure, or both. One man, a ship's cook, had died in the lifeboat, but all remaining fifty-five soldiers and sailors survived their ordeal. In the meantime, Commander Yokota had taken the *I-26* north along the coast to Vancouver Island, British Columbia, and further action. The American press was not told the truth about the sinking of the *Coast Trader*, nor of any of the other American vessels attacked or sunk by Japanese submarines along the west coast. It was considered not to be in the interests of public morale at the time to admit that the US Navy was virtually powerless to prevent Japanese submarines from coming so close to the coast of the United States. Already, the bombardment of the Ellwood oil refinery in California by Lieutenant-Commander Kozo Nishino and the *I-17* in February had sparked rumours of an imminent Japanese invasion. Officially, the destruction of the *Coast Trader* was the result of an 'internal explosion' aboard the ship, and not the impact of a Japanese Long Lance torpedo. Incredibly, this position remains on file in Washington DC today as the 'official' cause of the loss of the vessel, even though Commander Yokota himself reported torpedoing and sinking an enemy vessel on a date and at a location exactly matching that of the *Coast Trader* when the *I-26* returned to Yokosuka, Japan on 7 July 1942.

Now it was the turn of Canada to be attacked by the Japanese on her own doorstep, though the target for shore bombardment was incongruous to say the least. Vancouver Island forms part of the huge Canadian province of British Columbia, lying in the Pacific Northwest. The shoreline is dotted with numerous lighthouses that have for generations guided the local fishing fleets, as well as trans-Pacific telegraph stations vital to late nineteenth through to mid-twentieth century international communications. Estevan Point lighthouse was constructed in 1909, and is one of the oldest Euro-Canadian structures in the region, standing in 1942 close to a local Indian settlement called Hesquiat. It was a relatively remote area little affected by the Pacific war, but all that was rudely shattered in the late evening of 20 June 1942 by the Japanese submarine *I-26*.

Commander Minoru Yokota surfaced his boat approximately two miles out at sea directly off the lighthouse and ordered his gunners to pump shells at the building in the hope of toppling the structure. Only twenty-eight years before the whole Canadian Pacific coastline had been placed under the protection of the Imperial Japanese Navy, but now they had come to spread destruction in this quiet backwater. In 1914, when Canada united with the rest of the Empire and declared war on Germany in response to Britain's declaration, the nation's attentions and its limited naval forces were concentrated upon the conflict in Europe and the protection of the Atlantic seaboard. The Pacific was not the central theatre of war, and although a German threat existed as the Kaiser maintained a number of colonies throughout the region, Britain's ally, Japan, was able to deal with this latent threat. Canada recognized that the trans-Pacific telegraph stations were vulnerable to German attack, as a German naval landing party had cut the telegraph at Fanning Island early in the conflict, and the Canadians stationed what troops they could spare to defend the stations located on Vancouver Island. The Japanese stepped into the breach and offered to provide naval forces to patrol and protect the Canadian Pacific coast from any German intervention, and Ottawa gratefully accepted this offer. The Japanese stationed a heavy cruiser, the *Izumo*, in Canada at Bamfield on the west coast of Vancouver Island. By 1942, however, the earlier friendship between Canada and Japan had dissolved, with hundreds of Canadian soldiers being killed, wounded and taken into a cruel captivity following the Battle of Hong Kong in December 1941.

Yokota's shelling of the lighthouse at Estevan Point has recently come under historical scrutiny in Canada, and the lighthouse attack has become a controversial issue. According to the Canadian government, the *I-26* fired between twenty and thirty 140mm rounds from her deck-gun at the lighthouse, but caused almost no damage before leaving the area after an hour sitting on the surface offshore. There are those who doubt whether the attack was the work of the Japanese, and these 'conspiracy theorists' have suggested that the shells actually originated from an American ship or submarine, and intentionally failed to cause any material damage. The harmless attack was made, according to the revisionist historians, in an effort to bolster Canadian Prime Minister Mackenzie King's Liberal government that found itself in the midst of a controversial move to implement conscription in Canada. Historians writing in Canada's foremost history magazine *The Beaver* suggest 'The timing of the submarine attack seems like a stroke of phenomenal luck for...King, the Liberal party, and, possibly, even the continued unity of Canada. Or was the timing a little too perfect?'[13] The authors noted that the debate on the controversial conscription bill was at that moment raging in parliament in Ottawa. 'Perhaps a discreet "enemy incident" of the manufactured sort was just the thing needed to galvanize Canadian public opinion toward the kind of all-out effort needed to justify overseas conscription.'[14] According to post-war statements made by Commander Yokota, skipper of the *I-26*, chief gunner Hashiro Hayashi took aim on the lighthouse at a range of two miles and commenced firing at 10.15 p.m. on 20 June. Although approximately twenty to thirty shells, accounts vary, were fired at the very prominent and tall target, not a single round struck either the lighthouse or the nearby Indian settlement. This incredibly poor gunnery has provided conspiracy theorists with evidence for an American firing the shots instead, and deliberately missing the human habitation and important navigational beacon whilst posing as an enemy intruder. Yokota explained that the appalling marksmanship of his gunners was 'because of the dark, our gun-crew had difficulty in making the shots effective'.[15] The revisionist historians who challenge the very presence of the *I-26* point out that even at the time of the attack, 10.15 p.m. on a late June evening at such a latitude, 'it would have been still light enough to read a newspaper'.[16] They also suggest that Yokota was 'honour-bound to corroborate any official statement made by the newly established authorities, the victorious Allies'.[17] There are certainly some inconsistencies that have allowed doubts as to the veracity of the attack to creep into the frame. The lighthouse keeper, Robert Lally, made a note in his log during the attack of two 'warships' firing on Estevan Point from two different directions. In all later government reports the two warships were reduced to one submarine. The official report submitted by the senior Canadian naval officer in the Pacific to the government in Ottawa in July 1942 stated that the bombardment 'was in all probability carried out by one submarine mounting 5.5-inch guns forward of the sub's conning tower'.[18] However, Japanese I-class submarines such as the *I-26* were fitted with a single 140mm (5.5-inch) gun mounted behind the conning tower. American submarines, on the other hand, match the Canadian officer's description of the offending vessel perfectly, and American boats were the only other submarines operating in that region at that time.

On 3 July 1973 an unexploded Japanese Navy 140mm shell was discovered close to Estevan Point. Although Canadian bomb disposal experts destroyed the shell, a fragment survives and is on display at the Maritime Museum of British Columbia. This physical hard evidence of the Japanese attack goes some way to disproving some sort of elaborate subterfuge being played out on the Canadians by the United States in order to solidify Canada's resolve regarding a full commitment to the war in Europe. But, the claims made by some Canadian historians are also compelling. After all, why did Yokota select such a militarily and economically irrelevant target as an old lighthouse to bombard when his contemporaries making similar attacks along the American west coast attacked a naval base and an oil refinery? Perhaps it was not the target that was important – after all, how much damage could a single Japanese submarine cause to any shore target? Surely the mere suggestion that Japan was capable and willing to attack land targets in the United States and Canada is the point. The attacks primarily were designed to spread fear and panic among the citizenry of those two nations and not to cause extensive damage. The debate over the Estevan Point attack may rumble on for many years to come, with the truth perhaps always remaining elusive. Yokota went to his grave adamant that he had indeed shelled Canadian soil, and performed the mission he had been assigned.

The unique Japanese attack on Fort Stevens in northern Oregon on 21 June 1942, noteworthy as the first enemy attack on a military target located on the mainland of the United States since the conclusion of the War of 1812 at New Orleans in 1815 (Commander Nishino in the *I-17* had already claimed the first attack of any kind made upon the mainland when he shelled the Ellwood Oil Refinery in California on 23 February 1942 against direct orders issued by Admiral Nagano), resulted from an order from Rear-Admiral Shigeaki Yamazaki, commanding the 1st Submarine Squadron. Yamazaki's order demonstrated an about-face in Japanese strategy, following on from Colonel James Doolittle's air raid on Tokyo on 18 April. The Japanese had been completely surprised by the appearance in the skies over their capital city of stripped down B-25 Mitchell bombers. The tiny tonnage of bombs dropped from these medium bombers only caused very superficial damage, but the propaganda value of the raid to the Allies was immense and the Japanese high command immediately dropped all reservations regarding shelling American and Canadian shore targets from submarines. The humiliation of 18 April had to be avenged, and submarines were the only assets the Japanese possessed at that time able to come close enough to the North American mainland to strike at the hated enemy home front. The Japanese government also hastily drew up some new laws prohibiting certain forms of attack against their people and property that were actually used to murder or punish unfortunate Allied aircrew that fell into their hands. It became punishable by death or ten or more years imprisonment to commit any of the following offences:

Any air attack,

(1) upon ordinary people

(2) upon private property of a non-military nature

(3) against other than military objectives

(4) 'violations of war-time international law'.[19]

The two air attacks conducted by Fujita against Oregon in 1942 violated Japanese military law on the first three counts listed above. But the Japanese military and navy already had broken just about every aspect of international law since 1937 with impunity.

The *I-25* began her third war patrol on 11 May 1942, departing from Yokosuka in Japan in company with her sister-vessel, the *I-26*. Both were bound for a patrol along the north-west coast of the United States. As related earlier, only the *I-25* carried an E14Y1 reconnaissance aircraft in her watertight deck hanger, the *I-26*'s hanger was left deliberately empty. Both boats had a vitally important role to play in the Japanese attack on Midway Island, Operation Mi. The Japanese Midway operational plan called for a diversionary attack to be made on Dutch Harbor in Alaska, in the hopes of drawing off American aircraft carriers and other warships from the vicinity of Midway Island. On 27 May the *I-25*'s floatplane, piloted by the redoubtable Chief Warrant Officer Nobuo Fujita, conducted a successful reconnaissance flight over Kodiak Island, spotting an American cruiser and two destroyers. After the successful recovery of Fujita (the *I-26*'s hangar had been kept empty just in case the *I-25* had been unable to recover the floatplane), the *I-25* sailed on down the west coast of America, arriving off the coast of Oregon on 14 June. While off the Oregon coast the *I-25* launched a series of false submarine periscopes constructed of painted bamboo, which were mounted on special submerged rafts, designed to confuse local American anti-submarine forces that were conducting regular patrols along the coast.

On 18 June, Lieutenant-Commander Tagami, commanding officer of the *I-25*, received new instructions from Rear-Admiral Yamazaki, ordering him to attack American military targets along the west coast by shelling them with his deck-gun. The *I-26* received the same instructions at the same time, and went on to attack the Estevan Point lighthouse in Canada on the evening of 20 June, as related before. Just after midnight on 20 June 1942 Commander Tagami in the *I-25* came upon the brand new British freighter *Fort Camosun* approximately seventy miles south-south-east of Cape Flattery.

The *Fort Camosun* was on her maiden voyage from Victoria, British Columbia, to the United Kingdom loaded with zinc, lead, plywood and an assortment of other raw materials. Tagami lined the *I-25* up for a shot and fired a single Long Lance torpedo at the freighter. The torpedo struck the *Fort Camosun*, and as the merchantman slowed to a halt Tagami ordered the *I-25* to surface. He intended to finish off the freighter with his deck-gun in order to conserve his very limited supply of torpedoes, and several armour-piercing shells slammed into the badly damaged ship causing further mayhem.

In the meantime, the radio operator had managed to get off a distress call that was picked up by the Royal Canadian Navy. The corvette HMCS *Quesnel* immediately set sail for the scene of the attack, a journey that would take her six hours to complete. In the meantime the *I-25* had once more submerged and Tagami was monitoring his victim through the periscope, expecting the *Fort Camosun* to succumb to her injuries and sink at any moment. When the *Quesnel* arrived at the scene she immediately attacked the Japanese submarine, and shortly afterwards another Canadian corvette, HMCS *Edmunston*, joined in the attack and attempted to screen the *Fort Camosun* from the lurking Japanese submarine while her crew were taken off. Tagami realized the danger his boat was in with two anti-submarine corvettes in the area and wisely decided to withdraw. Incredibly, twenty-four hours later the *Fort Camosun* was still afloat, possibly buoyed up by the tons of plywood packed into her holds. The *Edmunston* took the freighter under tow, but was unable to haul the large ship to shore by herself. Three tugs joined in the effort to save the *Fort Camosun*, the *Henry Foss* out of Tacoma, Washington, the *Salvage Queen*, and the USS *Tatmuck*. Between them they gingerly towed the *Fort Camosun* into Neah Bay. Her journey to the dockyards and extensive repairs would take her first to Esquimalt in British Columbia, then to Victoria, and finally into Seattle. The *Fort Camosun* survived her ordeal at the hands of the *I-25*, and later in her career survived another torpedo strike, this time in the Gulf of Aden.

After the unsuccessful attack on the British freighter on 20 June, Tagami arrived off the mouth of the Columbia River the following day. Japanese naval intelligence had informed the *I-25*'s skipper that there was a US Navy submarine base located at the port of Astoria, close to the river mouth. However, lying between the *I-25* and her intended target was the huge Fort Stevens. Work had begun on constructing Fort Stevens in 1863 in the middle of the American Civil War, after President Abraham Lincoln expressed his concern that Confederate (and British) privateers operating in the Pacific could theoretically have raided towns lying along the Columbia and Willamette Rivers. Something needed to be done to protect the entrance to the Columbia, and the result was the construction of three forts named Stevens, Columbia and Canby, each made up of several emplaced gun batteries, Stevens being the most extensive. Although not to see any action during the Civil War (the fort was not fitted with cannon until shortly after the conclusion of hostilities in 1865), Fort Stevens nevertheless provided a formidable obstacle for any seaborne raider attempting to penetrate the Columbia River.

Time passed, and the weapons at the three forts were progressively upgraded and modernized; some of the batteries were closed down especially during the lean inter-war years, and National Guardsmen continued to man and train on the fortifications. The defences were never tested for real until Commander Tagami and the *I-25* hove into view on the night of 21 June 1942. Fort Stevens was fitted with many types and calibres of artillery, all of it dating from the turn of the century. There were 6-inch and 8-inch guns, and 12-inch mortars. One of the most novel weapons mounted on the fort were 10-inch rifles, a particularly impressive and innovative gun. Each time the weapon was fired the barrel would recoil backwards to an automatic locking-point, which meant that the weapon actually disappeared inside its embrasure allowing the crew to reload the rifle out of sight of the enemy. Not surprisingly, this weapon was nicknamed the 'Disappearing rifle'. Fort Stevens contained enough firepower to stand off a Japanese fleet, let alone a single puny submarine armed with nothing more impressive than a 140mm deck-gun.

Protecting the mouth of the Columbia was a ring of electrically controlled mines anchored below the water's surface at selected depths. A total of 156 mines were arranged into twelve groups of thirteen, each group linked to a control room in the fort by cables.

A final deterrent to a potential enemy were Sperry searchlights mounted on the fort. Each searchlight was enormously powerful, able to illuminate a ship at a maximum range of six to eight miles, doubly important to the fort because it lacked radar (all radar sets had been allocated to the army for anti-aircraft duties).

Sunday, 21 June was the longest day of the year. The air was warm as the *I-25* slowly and discreetly trailed fishing boats heading into the approaches to the Columbia River in the darkness. A myriad of lights twinkled and glittered from the shore, indicating to the Japanese officers on the conning tower the town of either Astoria or Seaside. The wind was a mere 4 knots, which meant that the sea was calm and therefore Warrant Officer Sensuke Tao, the boat's chief gunner, should not have encountered undue difficulties hitting his target. Indeed, down on the deck, Tao was overseeing his gunners as they prepared the weapon for action, the barrel pointing up at thirty to forty degrees, all ready to begin pumping rounds onto the American shore.

All three forts, Stevens, Columbia and Canby, were in telephone contact with each other. As reports of vessels out at sea were made by visual observation, this information was passed around the forts. As the *I-25* silently drifted across the entrance to the Columbia River, approximately 20,000 yards offshore, the troops manning the batteries expected another quiet and uneventful watch. Commander Tagami gave the order to commence firing, and with a wave of his hand Warrant Officer Tao fired the first shell landward. As the first Japanese shells began exploding around Fort Stevens all hell broke loose. At Fort Columbia, Corporal Patrick Jordan was the senior NCO still on duty. Inside the duty office there were two black telephones, the alert phones, and one of these began ringing. The voice at the other end was excited, and exclaimed 'Fort Stevens is under fire, sound your alert!'[20] Jordan could not believe his ears, and replied, 'What the hell did you just say?'[21] to which the soldier repeated himself more urgently. Jordan quickly put through a call to the off-duty senior NCO, First Sergeant Swaggert, 'I just got a call from Fort Stevens,' he said, 'and they said Fort Stevens is under fire, sound the alert.'[22] Swaggert took the news calmly, and barked back at

Jordan, 'Well sound the God damn alert!'[23] Jordan rushed outside to where there was positioned a large hand-operated air raid siren, which he began cranking with alacrity.

Soon the night air, already rent by the whistle and loud bangs of the incoming Japanese shells was further disturbed by the mournful wail of the siren, as troops rushed to man their positions and prepared to return fire. Fort Stevens, however, was destined not to fire a single shot in reply to the *I-25*'s bold attack. The Senior Duty Officer at the Group Fire Control Station in charge of ordering the batteries to fire, Captain Robert Huston, refused to give the order. As far as Huston could tell there were three problems that prevented him from unleashing the fort's considerable firepower at the Japanese interloper. Firstly, from the distant muzzle-flash of the Japanese deck-gun Huston estimated that the enemy vessel was approximately 20,000 yards from the fort. Although the 10-inch rifles mounted on the fort were much more potent weapons than the puny 140mm (5.5-inch) Japanese gun, the antiquated nature of the fort's armament meant that the rifles could only shoot a maximum of 16,200 yards. Secondly, the enemy vessel appeared to be moving and firing, and Huston lacked radar with which to accurately control his fall of shot onto the target, assuming the enemy vessel came within range. Thirdly, and perhaps rather ignominiously, Huston believed that if he ordered the batteries to open fire the Japanese would easily pinpoint the muzzle-flashes from the big 10-inch rifles, and begin a form of counter-battery fire on the fort's main armament. As the rifles were out of range the Japanese gunners could have hit the American gunners with impunity. In the meantime, confused American gunners stood by their weapons wondering when on earth their officers would issue the order to open fire. Morale began to plummet among the ordinary American soldiers as Japanese shells continued to impact around the fort. Corporal William Wilson, operating a searchlight that night, noted a general feeling amongst the other ranks of 'here we're fired on, why can't we fire back?'[24]

The lack of an American response to the Japanese shells was not helpful to the *I-25*'s gunners. Although there were lights ashore, the Japanese had little idea of what they were actually shooting at, and simply poured shells in the general direction of Fort

Stevens. The attack was more psychological than military after all, demonstrating the impunity with which the Japanese could strike at the mainland United States. The *I-25* fired seventeen shells, causing only superficial damage ashore, before quietly departing the area and heading for Yokosuka in Japan where she arrived on 11 July 1942. As for Fort Stevens, the antiquated nature of her armaments and a lack of radar demonstrated that the enormous potential firepower of the facility was in fact powerless, and was easily outsmarted by a single enemy warship. It was only by sheer luck that the Japanese gunners did not strike anything important on land with their wild barrage of random shells. If this little battle had occurred in daylight Fort Stevens would still have been unable to make a reply to the impudent Japanese intruder, and the Japanese gunners would have probably been able to target specific locations with ease. Nevertheless, as another demonstration of 'hit and run' tactics being employed to unsettle the American west coast it was very successful. On three separate occasions, 17 April, and 20 and 21 June Japanese submarines had come close enough to the coast of North America to land shells, and it was really a miracle that more serious damage had not been caused by the indiscriminate barrages. On all three occasions no response had been made to the Japanese raiders, no aircraft or anti-submarine ships had arrived at the scene, even though each submarine had remained at the surface for a considerable period of time as the crews busily fed shells into their gun. The impunity the Japanese evidently felt when striking at the mainland assisted them greatly in the planning of more audacious aerial attacks on the United States, stretching the offensive potential of their big I-boats to the full limit.

Notes

1. Colin Smith, *Singapore Burning: Heroism and Surrender in World War II*, (London: Viking), 2005
2. Donald J. Young, *Phantom Raid on L.A., World War II*, September 2003
3. ibid.
4. ibid.
5. ibid.
6. Burt Webber, *Silent Siege: Japanese Attacks against North America in World War II*, (Fairfield: Ye Galleon), 1984
7. Steve Horn, *The Second Attack on Pearl Harbor: Operation K and Other Japanese Attempts to Bomb America on World War II*, (Annapolis: Naval

Institute Press), 2005
8. Data derived from Bob Hackett & Sander Kingsepp's *HIJMS Submarine I-23: Tabular Record of Movement*, http://www.combinedfleet.com/sensuikan.htm
9. Mark Felton, *Yanagi: The Secret Underwater Trade between Germany and Japan, 1942–1945*, (Barnsley: Pen & Sword Books Ltd.), 2005, p.20
10. Horn, op. cit.
11. *Attack on the SS Coast Trader*, California State History Museum, California State Military Department, http://www.militarymuseum.org
12. Donald J. Young, '*West Coast War Zone*', *World War II*, http://historynet.com
13. *Edmonton Journal*, 2 April 2004
14. ibid.
15. ibid.
16. ibid.
17. ibid.
18. ibid.
19. Lord Russell of Liverpool, *The Knights of Bushido: A Short History of Japanese War Crimes*, (London: Greenhill Books), 2005, p.71
20. *Harbor Defenses of the Columbia River During the Second World War*, http://www.csus.edu
21. ibid.
22. ibid.
23. ibid.
24. ibid.

Chapter 6

Target Sydney

When you receive this letter you will know that I was killed in the Australian area on 31 May. I have nothing to regret. Today I will enter [censored] harbour in order to strike an enemy battleship. Take care of my parents and sisters.

Petty Officer Masao Tsujuku, midget submarine navigator, Sydney attack

A man may journey to a place he knows, but it takes men of rare courage to go to a place from which there is little hope of return.

Tatsuo Kawai, former Japanese Minister to Australia, June 1942[1]

Japan knew little of Australia when she started her war with the United States and the British Commonwealth. The Japanese rapidly conquered vast stretches of south-east Asia and the Pacific, perhaps beyond even their own expectations, and before long Australia was virtually on the southern frontline of the new Japanese Empire. Australia was an important member of the British Commonwealth, and she had immediately joined Britain in declaring war against Germany in September 1939, and then Italy and Japan as each new foe appeared and the war in Europe spread to the entire globe. The Japanese Navy saw that Australia held the potential to become a vast base and staging area for Anglo-American armies that could directly threaten the Japanese possessions in south-east Asia. On 10 January 1942 the Imperial General Headquarters-Government Liaison Conference in Tokyo concluded in its report with two important points of policy to be applied to the threat posed by Australia. Firstly, the Japanese Navy would have to isolate Australia by cutting her lines of communication with India, Britain and the United States.[2] Such a confinement would require Japanese submarines to actively interdict the seaways used by Australia to communicate and trade with the rest of the world; a serious undertaking when one considers the size of the Australian continent and the small submarine force available to the Japanese. Secondly, the navy would have to seal Australia off from the other Allied powers, and prevent troops and ships from making it to Australia in the first place.

The Japanese planned three actions in accordance with their outlined general plans concerning Australia, utilizing both air and sea power. Firstly, air attacks were to be directed against the closest large Australian city that could be reached by Japanese planes: Darwin. Secondly, air and ground attacks would be launched against Port Moresby in New Guinea, and thirdly, midget submarine attacks were to be launched against the important Allied naval base in Sydney Harbour. Japanese submarines would also support this operation by conducting shore bombardments and the interdiction of coastal merchant ships. This chapter deals with the submarine element of the overall Japanese strategy enacted against Australia in 1942, the midget and I-class submarine attacks on Sydney, Newcastle and inshore commerce. Before the Japanese launched the daring midget submarine raid into Sydney Harbour, submarine-borne Japanese spotter planes took to the skies over Australia searching for enticing targets for the fleet.

Kwajalein in the recently captured Marshall Islands had become the base for the Japanese 6th Fleet, the Imperial Navy's submarine force. Vice-Admiral Mitsumi Shimizu, based aboard the flagship *Katori*, a light cruiser, commanded the 6th Fleet. The fleet was subdivided into six squadrons, each under the command of a rear-admiral. Each submarine squadron consisted of several submarine divisions, totalling twenty-one in all. In each submarine squadron a light cruiser acted as a flagship, and each submarine division normally contained three or four submarines, a division being commanded by a captain. The *I-25*, which was to be engaged against the American mainland as well as Australasia, belonged to the 1st Submarine Squadron, along with the fleet boats *I-9, I-15, I-17, I-19, I-23* and *RO-61* and *RO-62*.

On 8 February 1942, a week after sustaining superficial damage in an American carrier plane strafing attack on the 6th Fleet anchorage, the *I-25* departed on her second war patrol. Admiral Shimizu ordered Lieutenant-Commander Tagami to take his boat to the east coasts of Australia and New Zealand, and using the Yokosuka E14Y1 floatplane carried aboard, to launch a series of reconnaissance missions over important Allied naval bases and commercial shipping centres, such as Sydney and Melbourne, gathering intelligence for future Japanese attacks in the Antipodes. Conventional submarine hunting was not prohibited on this mission, and Tagami struck on 14 February close to the north-east coast of Australia, sinking the 5,104-ton British freighter *Coldbrook* with torpedoes.

One of the main civil defence problems confronting the officials responsible for the defence of Sydney was a marked unwillingness of many of the inhabitants of the city to take air raid precautions seriously. For example, on 14 January 1942 an air raid alert and blackout was sounded throughout the city, and this led to 707 persons being discovered flouting the blackout. On 11 February a drill was sounded again, but this time the number of blackout offenders had grown to 822, indicating that all over Sydney lights remained burning fiercely, providing any incoming enemy aircraft with useful navigational and targeting points. As civil defence units attempted to deal with civic disobedience a very real threat materialized out to sea close to the city.

On the night of 14 February the Japanese submarine *I-25* motored quietly on the surface in the swell, Commander Tagami and his officers watching searchlights play across the sky above the city, numerous pinpricks of light twinkling in the distance indicating uncovered windows and unshielded car headlights. Tagami ordered the *I-25* to a new position 100 miles south of Sydney, a less conspicuous location where the planned aerial reconnaissance could be launched hopefully without interference. Arriving at the new location to find the sea pitching and rolling his submarine about, Tagami realized that it would prove impossible to safely launch and recover the Yokosuka floatplane to be piloted by Chief Warrant Officer Nobuo Fujita. Tagami would have to wait for the sea conditions to improve, and, in the meantime the *I-25* would remain undetected by the Australians, only coming to the surface in the dead of night to replenish her air supply and charge her batteries. For several days the *I-25* remained hidden beneath the waves during the hours of daylight, Tagami, his executive officer Lieutenant Tatsuo Tsukudo and Fujita poring over charts of the city, planning a daring flight over one of the Allies most important naval bases and commercial ports. By the evening of 16 February the sea had calmed sufficiently to allow Tagami to decide whether to launch Fujita on his reconnaissance mission over Sydney or abort the operation entirely. An hour after dark the *I-25* rose to periscope depth. Tagami completed a full sweep of the horizon, and satisfied that there was nothing out there except calm waters ordered his XO, Lieutenant Tsukudo, to surface the boat. The conning tower hatch was opened, allowing cool fresh air into the stale submarine, and officers and enlisted men scrambled topside to complete a further scan of the horizon with binoculars for any potential threats. The engineering officer was detailed to begin recharging the *I-25*'s batteries, using one of the large diesel engines, and to recharge the compressed air bottles. Both of these tasks were completed by midnight. In the meantime, Tsukudo took charge of the assembly of the E14Y1 floatplane, a job that normally took an hour to an hour and a half to complete. The timing of the mission was a crucial factor determining whether Fujita and his observer, Petty Officer Second Class Shoji Okuda, would regain the submarine following their sortie over enemy territory. If Fujita and Okuda were sent off too early they would return from their mission in the dark, making locating the *I-25* virtually impossible with the naked eye. Therefore, Tsukudo's mission plan gave Fujita one hour over Sydney, coupled with an hour's flying time to and from the target. Tsukudo decided that the floatplane would begin heading back to the *I-25* shortly after sunrise at 6.32 a.m. Although the submarine was vulnerable to attack when sitting on the surface in daylight, it remained the best chance for Fujita to pilot his aircraft back to the submarine and be successfully recovered. The aircraft, in several parts, was carefully removed from the *I-25*'s watertight hangar by a team of ten mechanics at 3.30 a.m. on 17 February. Under Tsukudo's expert supervision the mechanics assembled the floatplane ready for flight, scheduled to commence in one hour.

Fujita and Okuda boarded their assembled and fuelled float-plane and stared pointedly ahead at the sixty feet of catapult rail welded onto the submarine's deck that would serve as their runway. Commander Tagami turned his submarine into the wind and maintained a steady 18 knots, designed to assist the light floatplane into the air by providing extra lift as the catapult provided rapid acceleration.

Once airborne Fujita cruised the E14Y1 at a conservative 90 knots, and set course for Sydney Harbour. The Japanese aircraft crossed Botany Bay at about 7,500 feet, then banked to the north-west and crossed Parramatta. Dropping through low clouds to 5,000 feet, Sydney Harbour Bridge loomed out of the gloom below, whole sections of the harbour, despite repeated warnings concerning enemy air raids, well lit up. In particular, the powerful Macquarie Lighthouse remained operational, as well as the Garden Island naval base, including the large graving docks. In the glare of many lights across the harbour, Okuda was able to observe twenty-three Allied ships moored in the harbour or tied up alongside the docks, and among this number he discerned several large warships and five submarines.

Fujita and Okuda had seen enough, especially as light was beginning to filter into the sky around them, and their white fuselage and wings with blood red hinomaru rising sun roundels painted on them would soon attract attention from the ground as visibility improved. Although it was almost fully light by the time Fujita banked away towards North Head and the open sea, the Australian authorities had not registered the presence of a Japanese spotter plane over such a sensitive area. Fujita expected, at any moment, that a hail of anti-aircraft shells would fill the air around his plane, but there was no response from the ground at all. After passing over North Head Fujita dropped the floatplane down to about 150 feet above the surface of the sea and skimming the waves he set a course for his rendezvous with the *I-25*. As Fujita and Okuda flew slowly across the sea they spotted two merchant ships moving down the Australian east coast that would have made juicy targets for Tagami and his submarine, Okuda noting their position and course to pass on to his skipper when they returned.

Although Fujita arrived at the designated rendezvous point on time, the *I-25* was nowhere to be seen. Fujita was under strict instructions concerning maintaining radio silence, lest the Australians intercepted any Japanese transmissions and sent forces to hunt for the *I-25*. Fujita need not have worried, for when Okuda attempted to send a short radio message to the *I-25* he discovered that the radio was not working properly anyway. Low on fuel, Fujita had one option remaining before landing his plane in the sea: to conduct a limited grid search of the area in the hope of locating the *I-25*. Running practically on fumes, Fujita suddenly spied the Japanese submarine on the surface. To prevent a 'blue-on-blue', or so-called 'friendly fire' incident, as the aircraft approached the *I-25* Fujita waggled his wings to identify himself to the lookouts on the submarine's conning tower. In reply they released a yellow flare indicating the wind direction and requesting that Fujita land. Fujita executed a good landing into the sea and taxied alongside the *I-25*, where a retractable crane was used to haul the plane aboard for disassembly. Fujita and Okuda immediately briefed Tagami and Tsukudo on their mission, and by 7.30 a.m. the mechanics had successfully stowed the floatplane back in its hanger. Tagami ordered the *I-25* to proceed south on the surface at 14 knots, as Fujita and Okuda rested below after their challenging mission.

After successfully penetrating the airspace above Sydney Harbour, and remaining undetected and unchallenged by the Australians, Tagami's next task was to take his submarine to Melbourne and allow Fujita to conduct a similar reconnaissance sortie over the harbour. Entering the Bass Strait between Victoria and Tasmania on 18 February, Tagami would decide to launch Fujita from Cape Wickham, close to Melbourne's Port Phillip Bay. The Melbourne mission would prove to be a close run thing for Fujita and Okuda.

Throughout the morning of 19 February the *I-25* travelled on the surface some 200 miles east of the huge island of Tasmania, then the Japanese submarine turned south-east, taking the *I-25* to a position about eighty miles off the Cape Bruny lighthouse. During the afternoon the submarine battled through a major storm, pushing through heavy seas while heading west below Tasmania. By the following day the storm had begun to abate, allowing Tagami a moment to conduct his own reconnaissance before launching the floatplane on its mission. The *I-25* crossed the Bass Strait to Cape Otway, and, running at periscope depth ten miles off the coast, Tagami had a good view of the coastline of south-west Victoria. After making several sweeps of the Australian coast Tagami ordered the *I-25*'s periscope retracted, and the boat re-crossed the Bass Strait to Cape Wickham to prepare for the coming aerial mission. However, the sea conditions were still too choppy to risk launching the delicate floatplane, and in a repeat of the Sydney operation, the *I-25* was forced to wait out the bad weather until conditions improved.

Once darkness had fallen on 25 February Tagami determined that the sea conditions were now right to send Fujita and Okuda on their way. The *I-25* came to the surface and spent an hour navigating through reefs and shoals before reaching a position ten miles off Cape Wickham. The sea was calm, a light fog partially concealed the submarine and the white aircraft busily being assembled on its huge deck, and Fujita had a good navigational marker in the Cape Wickham lighthouse whose automated beam projected out to sea, an ideal point when searching for the submarine after completing the reconnaissance of Melbourne. Tagami turned the submarine's bows into the wind and increased the *I-25*'s surface speed to create an updraft to assist the E14Y1 into the air, and in the predawn darkness of 26 February the submarine's crew listened to the aircraft's engine sound fade into the fog as Fujita headed north across the Bass Strait towards Cape Otway. On reaching Otway, Fujita turned north-east and followed the coastline to another blazing lighthouse at Point Lonsdale at the entrance to Port Phillip Bay. Tearing through heavy cloud cover, Fujita took the floatplane north-north-east towards Portarlington. The heavy cloud cover proved to be a hindrance to Fujita's mission, as it was impossible for him to fix his position. As Fujita flew along the western shore of Port Phillip Bay at 4,500 feet he decided to rapidly descend and obtain an exact fix on his position before returning to the cover of the clouds. Dropping through the clouds the floatplane finally broke free at 900 feet, but when Fujita and Okuda pulled back the cockpit canopy and looked below panic immediately gripped them both. They had emerged directly above a Royal Australian Air Force base. RAAF Laverton was home to a dozen Wirraways, an armed Australian version of the American Harvard training aircraft, '...famous for its engine noise, which sounded uncannily like a motorbike'.[3] The base was also home to a few of the more potent Lockheed Hudson maritime bombers, each armed with six machine guns, and some Avro Anson trainers. Australian personnel on the ground spotted the low and slow flying Yokosuka floatplane, and a pair of aircraft were scrambled to attempt to intercept and shoot the interloper down. The cloud cover, which had proved such a problem for Fujita's navigation, now proved to be his salvation, as he immediately turned away from Laverton and into the clouds. Neither of the Australian aircraft located Fujita, who continued with his mission, though now much more wary of breaking cloud cover on the flight in to Melbourne to check his position. Okuda undoubtedly had taken to fingering the trigger on the single, rear-facing 7.7mm machine gun, the floatplane's only means of defence, though in the event of an entanglement with an enemy fighter both men knew the most likely outcome was a foregone conclusion.

Although appearing over an Australian airfield had proved alarming, Fujita next emerged from the clouds above Williamstown, close to a battery of four anti-aircraft guns. The gunners immediately identified Fujita's aircraft as Japanese, but in the excitement of actually being confronted by the enemy over home territory the officer commanding the battery decided to telephone headquarters for instructions instead of opening fire immediately. By the time permission had been granted to commence firing Fujita was gone, heading straight over the city of Melbourne without further challenge from the city's defences. From only 900 feet Okuda had an unobstructed view of the entire city and surrounding areas, as he eagerly leaned out of the cockpit with his binoculars. Okuda saw central Melbourne and the major dockyards at the mouth of the Yarra River, many houses and facilities showing lights even though the city was supposed to be under a 'brownout', with only essential lighting used and everything else switched off or blacked out. Okuda could even discern large flocks of sheep as their aircraft approached the city. Through his binoculars Okuda counted nineteen ships moored in Melbourne Harbour, and a light cruiser and five destroyers steaming into the harbour in a neat line.

Once again the regions' many lighthouses would prove to be excellent navigational beacons for Fujita as he banked his aircraft around the Cape Schanck lighthouse and headed back towards Cape Wickham. After passing over this lighthouse Fujita located the *I-25* without undue difficulty, landed, and the aircraft was smartly recovered from the sea and disassembled. Tagami now set a course to take the *I-25* back down the west coast of Tasmania on the surface. His next target for investigation was the port city of Hobart.

On Tasmania's east coast, close to the enormous island's waist, is located Great Oyster Bay, over twenty miles long and seven miles wide. Surrounded by impressive red granite cliffs and steep headlands, Commander Tagami decided to use this natural cover as the base from which to launch Fujita and Okuda on their third Australian sortie. The *I-25* slipped unnoticed into the moonlit bay on 1 March, and such was the seclusion offered by the location that Fujita requested that the floatplane be lowered into the water by crane, instead of the more usual high speed ejection along the *I-25*'s compressed air deck catapult. On a calm sea the little floatplane taxied clear of the submarine, and after a short run through the waves lifted clear into the sky trailing a great cloud of water spray draining from the surface of the floats as Fujita headed south towards Hobart.

After a while, he banked to the north-west and circled around the Tasman Peninsula, completing a final turn to approach Hobart from the south. Moonlight made ground identification relatively simple for Okuda, who spied only five merchant ships in Hobart's harbour, with no sign of any warships. Fujita made one pass and then turned about and retraced his route in to rendezvous with the *I-25*. When Fujita landed early morning light had appeared, and the crew were anxious to recover the plane and get on their way. Suddenly, the XO, Lieutenant Tsukudo, up on the conning tower, let out an exclamation and pointed to the south. A small freighter was lumbering her way along, and for a few moments all eyes turned to the distant vessel, followed by anxious moments as the submarine's crane was winched out over the floatplane, and the aircraft attached and made ready for winching aboard. The sea was becoming rougher, and as the crane took up the slack, and the aircraft began to lift clear of the water, the action of the waves on the floats caused Fujita's aircraft to pendulum backwards and forwards. With a nasty crunch a wooden wingtip connected with the crane arm. It was possibly a mission ending accident, for the *I-25* was unable to carry large spares such as aircraft wings. However, over the next four days, as the *I-25* made her way to New Zealand, the aircraft mechanics managed to patch the plane up sufficiently for Fujita to be able to take to the skies again, although Fujita voiced doubts about the plane's airworthiness nonetheless.

On 8 March Fujita and Okuda flew over Wellington, and this time the *I-25* herself courted disaster. Spotted by two Royal New Zealand Navy anti-submarine patrol boats, the Japanese submarine was slightly damaged during the subsequent depth charging she received. On the 12th Fujita took to the skies above Auckland, and then Tagami moved on to the British colony of Fiji. His target was the port of Suva, and on 19 March Fujita made a pass over the base, Okuda noting a British cruiser moored below them, before a searchlight illuminated their aircraft. Okuda thought fast, and grasping a signal light he flashed a meaningless Morse code message at the searchlight crew, who obligingly responded by switching their light off when confronted by what they evidently perceived to be a friendly aircraft. By 23 March the E14Y1 was in need of proper repairs, for when Tagami ordered Fujita aloft for a reconnaissance of Pago Pago the floatplane's engine refused to start. In the end Tagami had to resort to an inadequate periscope sweep of the island before heading for the Japanese naval base at Truk for fuel and provisions. The *I-25* then left for Japan, and a refit and overhaul at the Yokosuka Naval Base south of Tokyo.

Sunday is the traditional day of rest and 31 May 1942 found both the citizens of Sydney and many members of the crews from the collection of Allied warships drawn up in the harbour taking the day off and enjoying themselves. The cinemas, dance halls, restaurants and brothels of Sydney were all doing a good business from seamen on shore leave in the city. A feeling of unease, however, did permeate the fun, a feeling that the Japanese were coming to spoil the party. Nobody knew when and how the enemy may have arrived on the shores of Australia, but rumours of an imminent invasion abounded in the pubs and teashops, the newspapers and cinema newsreels fuelling the anxiety as Australians followed the progress of the Japanese advance towards their shores. The government of Prime Minister John Curtin had issued several warnings of an imminent Japanese attack on the continent since early 1942, fuelled by the deteriorating Allied situation in the Far East as the colonial powers, Commonwealth forces and the United States faced defeat after defeat from Hong Kong to the Philippines. At the time of the Japanese midget submarine attacks on Sydney Harbour, Australia appeared isolated and in imminent danger. Darwin, Derby and Broome in the north had all suffered heavy Japanese bombing raids. Malaya, Hong Kong and Singapore had all fallen to the seemingly relentless Japanese war machine, and thousands of Australian servicemen had become prisoners-of-war at the mercy of a contemptuous enemy. New Guinea was under heavy attack as Australian troops slogged it out with the Japanese along the Kokoda Trail as the Allies sought to hold onto Port Moresby. The Battle of the Coral Sea had been a close run thing for the United States and Australia. As Japanese submarines approached Sydney Australians felt their backs were against the wall, a feeling already experienced by their British cousins in the late summer of 1940, as Germany had seemed poised to invade across the English Channel.

On 10 April 1942 the commander-in-chief of the Japanese Combined Fleet had issued the following to the 6th Fleet, ordering the submarine units:

1. To reconnoitre the enemy's fleet bases in the Indian Ocean and the South Pacific
2. To destroy the enemy's maritime commerce
3. To lend support to the Port Moresby (MO) Operation.[4]

Submarines were immediately dispatched along with midget submarines from the tender *Chiyoda*, all coming under the designation Eastern Advanced Detachment (submarines *I-22, I-24, I-27, I-28* and *I-29*) and headed for Australia and New Zealand. The *I-29*, under Lieutenant-Commander Juichi Izu, arrived off Sydney on 13 May, and three days later attacked her first ship. Izu intercepted a Soviet freighter, the 5,135-ton *Wellen* fifty miles south-east of Newcastle, New South Wales, and launched two torpedoes at her. Both missed their target, so Izu surfaced the *I-29* and had his deck-gun brought into action. Japan and the Soviet Union were not at war at this time, so Izu's actions were dangerous and could have caused a diplomatic row with the one power Japan was keen not to antagonize. Although three Russian sailors were wounded, no significant damage was done to the Soviet ship, and Izu gave up and submerged.

The significance of this action was the suspension of all ship movements between Sydney and Newcastle for twenty-four hours, while a group of Australian corvettes searched in vain for the Japanese submarine. The *I-29* motored quietly back to Sydney and launched her aerial reconnaissance of the port. As a result of the *I-29*'s aerial reconnaissance of Sydney Harbour on 23 May, the Eastern Detachment Commander, Captain Hankyu Sasaki, ordered the force to begin making preparations to attack the large force of Allied warships noted to be in the harbour. Sasaki, aboard the *I-21* then engaged in reconnoitring the city of Auckland in New Zealand, sent a report of the reconnaissance mission to Admiral Komatsu, a radio transmission that was picked up and partially decoded by the joint US and Australian Navy's Fleet Radio Unit, Melbourne (FRUMEL). However, even though the Allies had broken the Japanese codes, no action was taken to stiffen the defences around Sydney. The *I-29*'s Glen float-plane piloted by Chief Warrant Officer Susumu Ito had recorded a collection of warships and merchant vessels inside Sydney Harbour. Ito and his observer had seen the heavy cruisers USS *Chicago* and HMAS *Canberra*, along with the light cruisers USS *Perkins* and HMAS *Adelaide*. Other warships in the harbour included the minelayer HMAS *Bungaree*, the armed merchant cruisers *Kanimbla* and *Westralia*, and the corvettes HMAS *Whyalla, Bombay* and *Geelong*. On 29 May a further aerial reconnaissance by an aircraft from the *I-121* revealed that the aforementioned enemy warships were still present, and the Eastern Advanced Detachment was given the go-ahead by Admiral Komatsu to attack the anchorage.[5] On this day both Komatsu and the detachment commander, Sasaki, sent radio messages of support and encouragement to the men who would undertake the assault on Sydney, and once again these communications were intercepted by FRUMEL and partly decoded. Once again, no action was taken to tighten security at the naval base in the light of obvious Japanese submarine activity close to Sydney.

Aboard the Japanese submarines *I-22, I-24* and *I-27* preparations were underway for the coming mission, the midget submarines carried aboard were being prepped and the crews briefed. The Japanese were waiting for the weak autumn sun to set, the midget submarine crews completing their final rituals before setting out to attack the enemy. All six men who would take the three midgets into Sydney Harbour that night were keyed up and also reflective about their chances of returning alive. Some quietly worshipped before small Shinto shrines erected inside the larger 'mother' submarines, following this with a farewell meal hosted by each submarine skipper. On board the *I-22*, the midget's navigator, Petty Officer Masao Tsujuku, carefully penned a farewell letter to his brother in Japan. Part of Tsujuku's letter read: 'When you receive this letter you will know that I was killed in the Australian area on 31 May. I have nothing to regret. Today I will enter [censored] harbour in order to strike an enemy battleship. Take care of my parents and sisters.'

The final time aboard the larger submarines was spent changing into clean uniforms and in performing the Way of the Tea ceremony. Following Shinto rites, the crewmen's bodies and souls were now clean. Clambering through the hatch connecting Midget *A21* to the submarine *I-22*, Lieutenant-Commander Ageta of the *I-22* was almost reduced to tears as he bade farewell to Sub-Lieutenant Keiu Matsuo and Petty Officer First Class Tsuzuku, urging both men to try and regain the *I-22* after completing their mission. For their part, Matsuo and Tsuzuku thanked Ageta for his efforts in bringing them this far and allowing them to undertake the coming mission. At 5.21 p.m. Midget *A21* began to motor towards the eastern entrance to Sydney Harbour, the crew of the *I-22* listening to their propeller sounds fading away into the night. The two crewmen of Midget *A14* aboard the *I-27*, Lieutenant Kenshi Chuman and Petty Officer First Class Takeshi Omori, had undergone similar rituals and farewells to Matsuo and Tzukuzu. At 5.28 p.m. their midget parted company with the *I-27* and set off for Sydney. Last to go was Sub-Lieutenant Katsuhisa Ban and his navigator, Petty Officer First Class Mamoru Ashibe, in Midget *A* at 5.40 p.m. from the *I-24*. Although their midget carried a number, that number remains unknown, so historians have referred to their craft as Midget 'A' since the attack. All three midgets motored the seven miles to the harbour entrance. At 7.45 p.m. Midget *A14* from the *I-27* slowly headed at periscope depth towards the entrance to the harbour, while the other two midgets waited.

The Sydney Harbour defences were not, according to the local anti-submarine officer, up to scratch. Acting Commander Harvey Newcomb had written to the Commodore-in-Charge, Sydney, Commodore Gerard Muirhead-Gould, warning him in January 1942 that enemy midget submarines could theoretically penetrate the harbour defences. Newcomb was a professional Royal Navy officer who had been dispatched from Britain in 1938 with orders to found an anti-submarine establishment at Edgecliff in Sydney. This facility had subsequently been named HMAS *Rushcutter*. In 1942 the means for detecting a submarine penetration of Sydney Harbour were in place. At the centre of the detection precautions were six electrical cables thousands of feet in length, laid on the seabed covering a wide expanse of the harbour approaches and entrance. Known as 'indicator loops', each cable would record electronically at a special shore station the passage of a ship or submarine over them. All contacts were automatically registered at the naval facility at South Head, close to the harbour entrance. The indicator loop system protecting the harbour was backed-up with an almost finished, and intended to be complete, anti-submarine and torpedo-net boom. One section of the net and boom could be opened and closed by small tenders, allowing vessels to enter the Harbour between Georges Head and Green Point. There were, however, some sizeable gaps in the net where the laying had not been completed by the time the Japanese attacked.

Newcomb's 20 January letter to Commodore Muirhead-Gould, who was also a Royal Navy officer, outlined concerns over efficient watch keeping and monitoring of the indicator loop system by naval personnel at South Head. In theory the harbour's early warning system allowed the Royal Australian Navy to combat any enemy penetration of the harbour, and careful